A Century of
CHAIR DESIGN

This book is to be returned on or before
the last date stamped below.

A Century of
CHAIR DESIGN

Editor
Frank Russell

Introduction
Philippe Garner

Drawings
John Read

ACADEMY EDITIONS

Acknowledgements
We express thanks to all the following contributors: Victor Arwas of Editions Graphiques London, Cavin O'Brien of Fischer Fine Art Ltd. London, Thomas A. Heinz, Liberty and Co. London, Sylvia Katz of the Design Council London, Marilyn Sparrow, Vicky Wilson.

Designed by Dennis Crompton

Front cover
BREUER Lounge chair, 1928, tubular steel frame with canework seat and back and wood armrests. The original version of this chair was manufactured by Standard-Möbel from 1928 until 1938; this model, together with a version in tubular steel and leather, has been in production since 1970.

Frontispiece
LE CORBUSIER Chaise longue, 1928. The chaise longue was the first to be made adjustable by simply moving the whole frame, which rests freely on the iron trestle. Originally manufactured by Thonet, it has been produced since 1965 by Cassina.

Back cover
BUGATTI Wood chair with vellum covered seat and back from a dining suite created for Bugatti's own use towards the end of his career.

First published in Great Britain in 1980 by Academy Editions 7/8 Holland Street London W8

First paperback edition 1985

ISBN 0-85670-858-5

Printed and bound in Hong Kong

Contents

Foreword

'In the end we shall sit on resilient columns of air.'

Sitting is an activity fundamental to everyday life, and if any item of furniture is indispensible, contrary to Marcel Breuer's dream of the future, it must be the chair. Perhaps because of this designers, especially architects, continue to find the chair a challenging design problem, imposing its own limitations and yet seemingly capable of an infinite variety of solutions. The aim of this book is to show the broad development of chair design between 1850 and 1950, a century of unprecedented technological change during which the transition from traditional methods of hand-craftsmanship to modern techniques of mass-production changed the appearance of the chair almost beyond recognition. The nineteenth-century side chair or dining chair made of wood and rush or leather to time-honoured and exacting standards of craftsmanship has been largely replaced in the twentieth century as an everyday chair in the home or office by simple architectonic feats in new materials like tubular steel or moulded ply, of which Breuer's 'Cesca' and Eames' lounge chair are fine examples. The century also witnessed the emergence of a number of ideological movements — Arts and Crafts, Art Nouveau, Art Deco and Modern, and designers have been grouped accordingly although in some cases their work will be found to fall outside the mainstream design of the period. In addition to the work of the great names we have come to associate with the chair, that of some lesser known craftsmen and designers has warranted inclusion, and it is hoped that this selection is varied enough for the reader to judge for himself what is of lasting value. There can be no doubt, whatever the time or temper, that a good chair is one which as far as possible expresses the ideal which recurs in the following pages 'fitness for purpose, truth to materials'.

    This book is a response to the need for a general survey of chair design in the recent past, and is the result of discussions with Philippe Garner, John Read, Dennis Crompton and the publisher Dr. Andreas Papadakis. The line drawings are by John Read, research on individual designers by Vicky Wilson. Our thanks go to all who have in some way contributed to this book.

Frank Russell

Opposite
BREUER 'Wassily' chair, 1925. The 'Wassily' chair, designed for the Bauhaus room of the painter Wassily Kandinsky, was the first chair in tubular steel, and has since become a classic of modern design.
Overleaf
MACKINTOSH Armchair, 1902.

Introduction

'A chair is a stool with a back-rest, and a stool is a board elevated from the ground by supports.' This definition is, perhaps surprisingly, that given by Dr Christopher Dresser in his chapter on furniture in *Principles of Decorative Design,* published in 1873. Dresser was an important pioneer of modern design but not even he could have anticipated the variety and novelty of chair design as it was to evolve over the next one hundred years. Perhaps he would have retracted his somewhat simplistic definition if he had seen chairs that were sacks of expanded polystyrene pellets, single units moulded in plastic or fibre-glass, or chairs constructed of inflated sausages of transparent P.V.C. Dresser's definition gives no hint of the cantilever principle, of the strength, flexibility and lightness, both visual and physical, that were gradually to be achieved through the development of ply and laminated woods, synthetic materials and new alloys. He was involved in the early phases of the evolution charted by Nikolaus Pevsner in his *Pioneers of Modern Design.* Within the story of this evolution, chair design acquired a quite special significance.

A chair, more perhaps than any other item of furniture, is subject in its design to the dictates of very specific requirements. Yet within these seemingly restrictive requirements there remains the potential for an infinite range of possible solutions. From a most utilitarian origin — as an object whose only variants were in the decorative treatment, according to the dictates of fashion, of a fairly rigidly accepted idea of structure — the chair became a statement of faith, the visual expression of new theories and ideals, the symbol of a new movement in the applied arts. The chair became a self-concious set-piece for the more avant-garde designer or architect, each introducing his own new concept of structure. In certain instances chair design became an almost obsessive cult. Charles Rennie Mackintosh was the first architect/designer for whom chair design became a highly important theme, and there are chairs that exemplify every phase, every subtle evolution in his work. The designers of the Bauhaus turned their energies towards the creation of an important series of chairs. During the late 1920s they designed the most significant group of chairs of the twentieth century, classics of modern design, their popularity and importance undiminished by subsequent developments. During the same period Le Corbusier, working with Charlotte Perriand, created a comparable nucleus of chairs which similarly enjoy a lasting popularity and which were conceived as the embodiment of strongly felt and still valid principles. Their celebrated chaise longue of 1928 expresses more succinctly, more eloquently than any number of Le Corbusier's published pages of theorising, his hope for a new future in design aligned finally to the realities, and, indeed, to the potential, of the machine age.

Often overshadowed by the creations of the great innovators, by designers such as Thonet, Mackintosh, Mies van der Rohe, Breuer, Le Corbusier, Aalto or Eames, there was a constant and at times fascinating production of decorative chairs reflecting prevalent fashions and, occasionally, in the hands of talented designers, achieving lasting recognition as perfect expressions of current ideals of taste.

COLLINSON Carved armchair presented at the
Great Exhibition.

Arts and Crafts

Within the hundred year span between 1850 and 1950 the history of chair design is marked by certain high points, an interesting and varied flurry towards the turn of the century, a period of increased momentum in the last twenty-five years and peaks of almost feverish activity, notably in the late twenties and the immediate post Second World War years. There is, similarly, a constant pattern of change in the focus of interest from one country to another.

England provides the most natural starting point for two reasons. It was in England that the ideological beginnings of the Modern Movement took root. But the best justification for looking to England is the Great Exhibition of 1851, the monumental assembly of 'the Industry of all Nations' which provides a revealing résumé of contemporary design and aspirations. Contemporary catalogues provide many illustrations of chairs, and the overriding impression is of well-upholstered opulence, and a passion for naturalism in the decorative treatment of the structure. This passion for naturalism was carried to an extreme, if logical, conclusion in a remarkable chair created by a Mr G. Collinson of Doncaster. The chair was constructed of lengths of wood carved in the form of lengths of branch, joined by entwined stems and leaves; wood carved to resemble wood. Amongst the most noteworthy chairs is the carved and inlaid walnut armchair made by Henry Eyles of Bath, bearing on its back an oval Worcester porcelain plaque painted with the full-length portrait of Prince Albert. The finely carved openwork surround is a hymn to the naturalistic style.

This naturalism is the strongest single thread linking chair designs exhibited from all over the world. Other notable features are the deep-buttoned upholstery and deep fringing that recur on so many exhibits. Carl Leistler, described by the *Art Journal* as the most important Austrian furniture maker, showed deep-buttoned chairs in massive carved locust wood. From the other side of the world came another interpretation of the same style in chairs by J.&W. Hilton of Montreal. Messrs. Hunter of London was one firm amongst many working in this favoured carved walnut, whilst the Birmingham firm of McCullum & Hodgson was singled out for praise for the production of chairs and other furniture in decorated papier-mâché.

The richly naturalistic and eclectic style of the Great Exhibition was the manifestation of a justly self-satisfied age. There was however a significant undercurrent of reaction which was soon to grow in strength and overshadow the early Victorian style, replacing it in avant-garde circles with a new idiosyncratic style, largely based on a reinterpretation of the Gothic and a rigid application of geometric principles to natural forms. The seeds of this new style had been sown well before the Great Exhibition by A.W.N. Pugin, an energetic and vigorous propagandist of the Gothic and a talented designer capable of injecting into it a new vigour. Pugin died in 1852 but the style continued to flourish and, by 1862 and the International Exhibition of that year, the Gothic style could be seen to be well entrenched. The seminal hand-book providing designers with a rich fund of decorative motifs was Owen Jones' *The Grammar of Ornament,* first published in 1856. The

McCULLUM & HODGSON

PUGIN Armchair, c.1840.

DRESSER Chair, c.1880.

GODWIN Side chair, 1885.

strictly formalised plant motifs of Jones' folio recur as decoration on chairs and other items of furniture. Dr Christopher Dresser's chair designs frequently incorporate inlaid or painted designs that owe a specific debt to Jones. Dresser was as concerned with structure as he was with decoration and in his 1873 analysis of chair design set down his key principles, with a fundamental emphasis on the need for truthfulness to the then current material for chair construction, wood. He decried the arch form in wood, contradicting as it did the natural strength in the straight grain. His own proposed designs show logic in their construction and he drew on other examples worthy of praise, notably an upright chair illustrated in Bruce Talbert's important but somewhat belated publication *Gothic Forms Applied to Furniture, Metalwork and Decoration for Domestic Purposes* of 1867. The design, praised for its 'admirable method of supporting the back', is an interesting precursor of Godwin's elegant Japonisant chair made by William Watt in 1885. The principle of logical construction survived, though in a new stylistic guise.

The successor to the Gothic revival was the cult of Japanese art which, until the early 1860s, was virtually unknown in Europe. What began as a collecting fad in fashionable artistic circles in Paris and London evolved into a new taste in design and decoration, notably in England, where it formed the basis of the so-called 'Aesthetic' Movement which was to reach the height of its success during the 1870s. Oscar Wilde's much publicised American tour made the movement's motifs, the sunflower and peacock feather, as popular on the other side of the Atlantic as they were in his own country. The most refined furniture designer in the new Anglo-Japanese style was E.W. Godwin. Manufactured by the London firm of William Watt, Godwin's designs were popular and much imitated. Characteristic features of the Aesthetic chair included wood turned to simulate bamboo, backrails of turned spindles, asymmetrical chequer backs, inlaid sprays of Japanese blossom but, above all, the slender ebonised structure that found its perfect expression through Godwin. In America the Herter brothers made their own version of the Aesthetic chair whilst the New York firms of C.A. Aimone, George Hunzinger and Kilian Brothers manufactured the popular imitation bamboo seat furniture.

Inextricably woven in with the Aesthetic Movement and, indeed, with the ideology of the Gothic revival, were the beginnings of the Arts and Crafts movement, the origins and guiding principles of which, in the writings of John Ruskin and William Morris, are already well known. The movement's central ideal was the re-establishment of craft workshops, an ideal derived from an unrealistic vision of the mediaeval age. Despite their democratic principles the Arts and Crafts practitioners became craftsmen to an élite, for there was no escaping the expense of hand labour, nor indeed the demand for a high standard of execution from the middle or upper class homes for which such productions were in fact destined. One is reminded of Marie Antoinette's supposed return to rustic simplicity in her hamlet in the gardens of Versailles. Morris's dream was as unrealistic as her finest porcelain milking pails.

MORRIS & CO. Kelmscott House, Hammersmith.

MORRIS & CO. Stanmore Hall, Harrow.

 MORRIS & CO. Rossetti chair.    GIMSON Clissett chair.   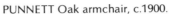 PUNNETT Oak armchair, c.1900.   SHAKERS Dining chair, c.1890.

The firm of Morris, Marshall, Faulkner and Co. was founded in 1861. Morris enlisted the talents of artist friends to design the furniture. D. G. Rossetti, for example, created a chair design, rush-seated, thin-membered, in ebonised wood, but very much a derivative of the old Sussex design, first adapted and introduced into production around 1865. This 'Sussex' chair was the most popular produced by Morris & Co. Another favourite was the upholstered, adjustable chair, adapted in 1865 from the design of a chair discovered by Warrington Taylor, the firm's manager, in an old Sussex carpenter's workshop.

Following in Morris's footsteps several Craft Guilds were established, coming together in the Arts and Crafts Exhibition Society, founded in 1888. The most notable talents to emerge from this Society were the designers and craftsmen of the Cotswold School, Ernest Gimson and Sidney and Ernest Barnsley. Combining a love of craftsmanship with a genuine knowledge of the principles of furniture design, theirs was the most independent and original contribution to the ideal of the movement. The most notable twentieth-century successors to the founders of the Arts and Crafts movement included Peter van der Waals for his design and craftsmanship and Gordon Russell for his more down-to-earth translation of the ideals of truth to materials and the natural beauty of the functional.

The natural immediate successor to the Arts and Crafts movement was a decorative mode concerned more with style than with ideals. There survive many chairs bearing witness to the success of this taste during the 1890s and early 1900s. Most often executed in oak they tend to have a self-conscious 'craft' look, often with specific mediaeval references, equally often intermingled with decorative motifs reminiscent of continental Art Nouveau. Perhaps the best example of the fashionable 'Arts and Crafts style' chair is the handsome design by E. G. Punnett made around 1900 by William Birch. Liberty and Co.'s label is to be found on many types of chair in this same vein.

Morris's teachings spread far and wide and nowhere were the guiding principles welcomed more readily than in America, where Gustav Stickley became the leading furniture maker of the new school. Under the trade-name 'Craftsman' Stickley devised a strong personal style, working largely in oak and with fitness for purpose as his overriding raison d'être of furniture design. Singling out a sturdy oak armchair, he wrote in 1909 'The fundamental purpose in building this chair was to make a piece which should be essentially comfortable, durable, well-proportioned and as soundly put together as the best workmanship, tools and materials make possible'. In the early years of this century the Roycroft Community workshops, East Aurora New York produced simple, sturdy oak chairs and other furniture very similar in style. In California the Greene brothers designed chairs, indeed entire houses, self-consciously exposing their pegged structure and displaying a strong oriental influence. Well worthy of study as an isolated example of the perfect integration of craft within a society are the American Shaker sect communities, whose simple, sturdy and well crafted designs were not subject to the whims of fashion but were a quasi-ritualistic part of community life.

STICKLEY Craftsman furniture, c.1910.

SHAKERS South family dwelling, New Lebanon.

1

2

3

4

The Great Exhibition

1851

The Great Exhibition or, to give it its full title, the Great Exhibition of the Industry of All Nations, was organised under the direction of Prince Albert for the purpose of 'exhibition, competition and encouragement' and held in Joseph Paxton's revolutionary glass and iron Crystal Palace. It was the largest, most lavish and best attended display ever assembled, and through its arrangement and introduction of international competition set the pattern for the international exhibitions that were to become a regular part of creative life in the second half of the nineteenth century and the first quarter of the twentieth. Although the British and Colonial section constituted over half the display the exhibition provided a comparative yardstick

through the inclusion of work from Europe and North America, and critics considered the British contribution to the applied arts, with the exception of Augustus Welby Pugin's Mediaeval Court, a failure in comparison to submissions from other countries. The furniture exhibited provides a useful survey of the taste of a period when Victorian naturalism had reached its apogee, and chair designs from all nations show a marked heaviness and reliance on semi-classical forms with a profusion of naturalistic carving and rich upholstery and decoration. This is exemplified in the chair by Henry Eyles, which relies for its effect on marquetry, carving and painted porcelain, rather than form.

Opposite
Drawing-room chair designed by Henry Eyles, walnut carved and decorated with marquetry and set with a painted porcelain plaque portraying Prince Albert. A companion chair with a portrait of Queen Victoria was also designed.
1   Drawing-room chair made by Gillow's of London.
2   Armchair designed by Carl Leistler of Vienna in locust wood with plush upholstery and elaborate carving. Leistler was already known to English critics through his furnishings for the Liechtenstein Palace (see illustration 9, page 57), and the 'furniture for a suite of palatial rooms' from which this chair is taken received much praise.
3, 4 Black walnut chairs covered in crimson and gold damask. Manufactured by J. & W. Hilton of Montreal.

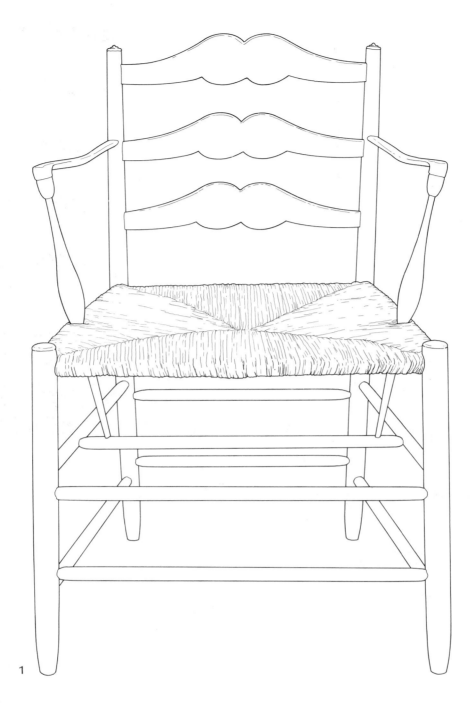

1

Ernest Gimson

1864-1919

Ernest Gimson was among the most devoted of British craftsmen to the ideals of the Arts and Crafts movement, and attempted to comply with its principles in both his life and work. He was very much influenced by William Morris, who obtained a post for him as apprentice in the London architectural practice of J. D. Sedding in 1886, and it was at Morris's suggestion that he began his first furniture making venture — Kenton & Co. — in collaboration with Sidney Barnsley, W. R. Lethaby, Reginald Blomfield, Mervyn Macartney and Colonel Mallet.

Although Gimson continued to work as an architect throughout his career, his major interest was the furniture workshops established in collaboration with Ernest

Barnsley in 1900, and located at Sapperton, near Leicester from 1902. Gimson's workshops epitomised the ideals of the Arts and Crafts movement, and as late as 1915 he refused the efforts of the Design and Industries Association to persuade him to design for industrial production, believing that his contribution to raising standards lay in the example of his work, and the sound training he gave his apprentices. Although he had a profound understanding of materials and techniques he made little furniture himself, concentrating on designing, making presentation drawings for clients and teaching. Peter van der Waals, a Dutch cabinet-maker, worked as chief cabinet-maker to the firm from 1901, and from 1904 the production of turned

rush-seated chairs was entrusted to Edward Gardiner.

Gimson allowed each craftsman to work on a piece from beginning to end to stimulate a sense of purpose and pride, and although it was his intention that the simple furniture produced should be cheap enough for ordinary cottagers, the high standards made this impossible, and clients were attracted from among his friends and architectural patrons and through exhibitions in London. His furniture was, however, cheaper than that of other similar concerns, and it is likely that he made little profit from his business.

The chairs manufactured to Gimson's designs draw their inspiration from traditional models, in particular the turned ash

2

3

rush-seated chairs, which were made in accordance with a technique which he learned in 1886 or 1887 from a Bosbury craftsman Philip Clissett. Gimson also worked in oak, usually left unpolished but occasionally treated with hot quicklime or stained black, and in walnut. His chairs have the simplicity of those of the Shakers, with honesty of construction and meticulous craftsmanship as their main criteria.

1 'Pass Chair', ash stained and polished with rush seat, executed by Edward Gardiner.
2 'Gimson Chair', turned ash with rush seat.
3 Walnut chair with drop-in rush seat.
4 The workshop at Pinbury Park which Gimson shared with the Barnsleys before moving to Sapperton in 1902.

4

1

Christopher Dresser

1834-1904

Christopher Dresser was one of the most important industrial designers of the second half of the nineteenth century, and a major influence through his lectures, work and writings on design and Japanese art. His belief that good design should be based on scientific knowledge rather than intrinsic cultural values represented a radical departure from current English Arts and Crafts theories, and his sparse, unornamented designs for metalware had an economy of form which made them ideal for industrial production.

Dresser trained at the School of Design in London, and subsequently worked as professor of Botany at several London institutions including the London Hospital Medical School. He began designing metalwork for firms in Sheffield and Birmingham in the 1860s, and subsequently designed ceramics, glassware, wallpapers and fabrics for many of the leading manufacturers of his day. In 1876 Dresser spent four months in Japan studying traditional Japanese methods of manufacture, and his subsequent work for the Linthorpe Pottery, which he founded in Middlesborough in 1876, shows the influence of Japanese and Chinese ceramics. His major contribution to furniture design was as editor of *The Furniture Gazette* in 1880 and artistic supervisor to the Art Furnishers' Alliance in London from 1880 to 1883.

Most of Dresser's furniture was designed during his period with the Art Furnishers' Alliance, and his principles were outlined in an anonymous letter to *The Furniture Gazette* contending that designers should 'give some thought to the purpose for which various pieces of furniture are required; the nature of the material of which they are to be made, the soundest and most economical methods of construction, the proportion of parts one to another and the effect when viewed as a whole, not forgetting the most legitimate way of ornamenting and finishing the work that they may be called upon to design'. His chair designs show a concern for solidity and soundness of construction combined with eclectic decoration, often Egyptian-inspired or grotesque, and reminiscent of his ceramic designs of the 1890s for William

Ault. The repetitive geometrical patterns echo the frieze and wallpaper designs published in his *Studies in Design* (1875) and *Modern Ornamentation* (1886).

1   Design for a hall chair, published in *The Furniture Gazette,* February 1880.
2   Design for a side chair, published together with a design for a couch using similar decorative motifs in *The Furniture Gazette,* January 1880.
3   Walnut armchair, c.1880, attributed to Dresser because of its similarity to the Bushloe House sofa.
4   Sofa, carved mahogany inlaid with ivory, ebony and other woods. Designed for Bushloe House, Leicestershire c.1880.

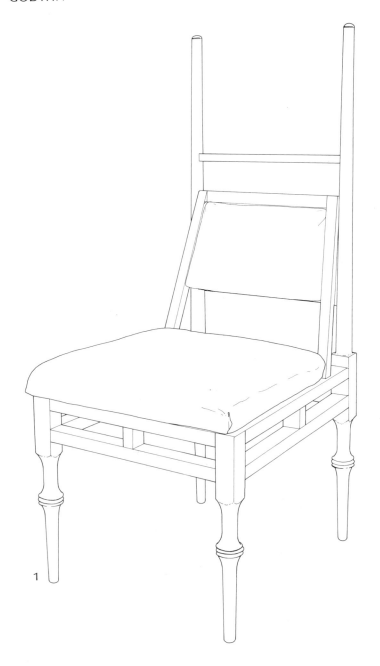

Edward William Godwin

1833-1886

1 Side chair, 1885, ebonised wood with upholstered seat and back.
2 Side chair, oiled wainscot oak with leather upholstery stamped in gold. Designed for Dromore Castle, Limerick.

Edward William Godwin was an English architect and designer of revolutionary simplicity and elegance, and one of the first artists to attempt the translation of Japanese ideas and forms into Western terms. The son of a Bristol decorator, he was articled to the Bristol City Surveyor William Armstrong before setting up his own architectural practice in 1854. His interest in Japanese art dated from about 1860, and in 1862 he decorated his own Regency house in accordance with Japanese taste. In partnership with Henry Crisp, Godwin designed town halls and country houses in the 1860s in a Gothic style as well as schools, houses and warehouses in the Bristol area. In 1865 he moved to London where he came into contact with

James McNeill Whistler, for whom he built the White House — a radically simple white cube — in 1877. He devoted his last years to stage design, furniture design and architectural journalism.

Godwin believed that furniture 'cannot be artistic work by any happy-go-lucky process', and his notebooks show considerable research into the structural details of mediaeval furniture, taken from manuscripts in the British Museum. His work also shows the influence of Japanese design in its elegant austerity, slenderness of parts, geometrical arrangement of straight lines and imaginative juxtaposition of solid and void. Godwin was one of the first designers to make extensive use of ebonised wood and bright mahogany, as in

the mahogany chairs upholstered in pale citron yellow designed for Whistler's 'Butterfly Suite' at the Paris 1878 exhibition.

As well as the chairs designed for his own buildings, such as Northampton Town Hall (1861-64) or Dromore Castle, Limerick (1866-73), which were manufactured by the Art Furniture Company, Godwin also designed furniture for several firms including William Watt, Gillow's, W. and A. Smee and Collinson & Lock, who at one time paid him a substantial monthly retainer. A survey of his work, which was much copied during his lifetime, can be found in Watt's catalogue *Art Furniture* of 1877, prefaced by an introductory letter by Godwin himself.

1

and Company

1 Oak settle with convex overhanging canopy and panels decorated with embossed leather paper. A cheaper version of this Philip Webb design with plain panels was also advertised in Morris & Co. catalogues.

son,
yn.

...e most influential en-
...nglish Arts and Crafts
...nded under the name
... Faulkner & Co. by
...1896) in April 1861.
rush   ...o form 'a company
etti.   ...xecute work in a
with   ...nd   inexpensive
own.   ...ll kinds of manu-
...y   ...', and he hoped
...d Inn,   ...and satisfying
... & Co.   ...d by closely
...George   ...n following
...uilds in their
...d oak   ...to nature.
...Philip   ...n alterna-
...1865.   ...chanical
...h seat   ...ted the

craftsman to a mere machine-minder, and encouraged the acceptance of poor quality work. The company expanded rapidly once Morris became sole proprietor in 1875, acquiring a prestigious Oxford Street showroom in 1877 and enlarged workshops at Merton Abbey in 1881. The furniture, wallpapers, fabrics, stained-glass and tapestries produced, however, were by no means 'inexpensive', and despite Morris's socialist views his interest was definitely in the selfish pleasure of creation rather than in helping 'the people' to attain a better standard of living. His collaborators during his lifetime included Ford Madox Brown, Edward Burne-Jones, Dante Gabriel Rossetti and Philip Webb, and the firm continued until 1940 when it went into

voluntary liquidation.

Although Morris designed no furniture for Morris & Co., and is reported by George Jack to have been 'somewhat indifferent about this part of his business', the furniture produced by the firm nevertheless conformed to his maxim 'have nothing in your house that you do not know to be useful or believe to be beautiful'. He himself made a distinction between 'the necessary workaday furniture' and 'state-furniture. . . as elegant and elaborate as we can with carving or inlaying or painting', and the firm was to produce both types throughout its existence.

The chairs belonging to the first category included adaptations of tradition-al designs such as the Sussex chair, and

2

3

4

much of the work of Ford Madox Brown. Madox Brown's designs were described in the *Arts and Crafts Exhibition Society Catalogue* of 1896 as having the qualities of 'adaptation to need, solidity, a kind of homely beauty and above all absolute disassociation from all false display, veneering and the like'. Madox Brown had been a designer in the early 1850s with George Seddon & Co., and his simple oak chairs use strong elementary forms reinforced by an appeal to traditional values, and rely on clearly expressed structure and honest if unspectacular workmanship. He is credited with the origination of green stain for oak furniture.

The other major designer working for Morris from the establishment of the com-

pany was Philip Webb, who designed and furnished Morris's own house, the Red House, Bexley in 1859. Webb was responsible for most of the larger, more elaborate painted furniture including a settle design with a convex overhanging canopy inspired by the work of Augustus Welby Pugin. His most famous piece was the adjustable chair of about 1865, which he adapted from a sketch sent to him by Warrington Taylor, the manager of the company, of a chair found in a Sussex carpenter's workshop.

From 1890, George Jack was chief designer, producing the Saville chair and a range of furniture in mahogany and rosewood with elaborate marquetry and metal mounts. Other designers producing furniture for Morris & Co. included

Rossetti, Holman Hunt, W.A.S. Be[n] Mervyn Macartney and Frank Brangw[yn]

2 'Rossetti' chair, stained oak with [rush] seat, designed by Dante Gabriel Ross[etti]
3 Round-seat chair in stained oak [with] rush seat designed by Ford Madox B[rown]
4 Oak armchair, 1876, designed [by] Richard Norman Shaw for the Taba[rd Inn,] Bedford Park and retailed by Morri[s & Co.]
5 Saville armchair, designed by [George] Jack c.1890.
6 Adjustable armchair, ebonise[d and] upholstered in velvet, adapted by [Philip] Webb from a traditional design [and] 7 Ebonised oak settle with ru[sh seat] belonging to the 'Sussex' series.

5

6

7

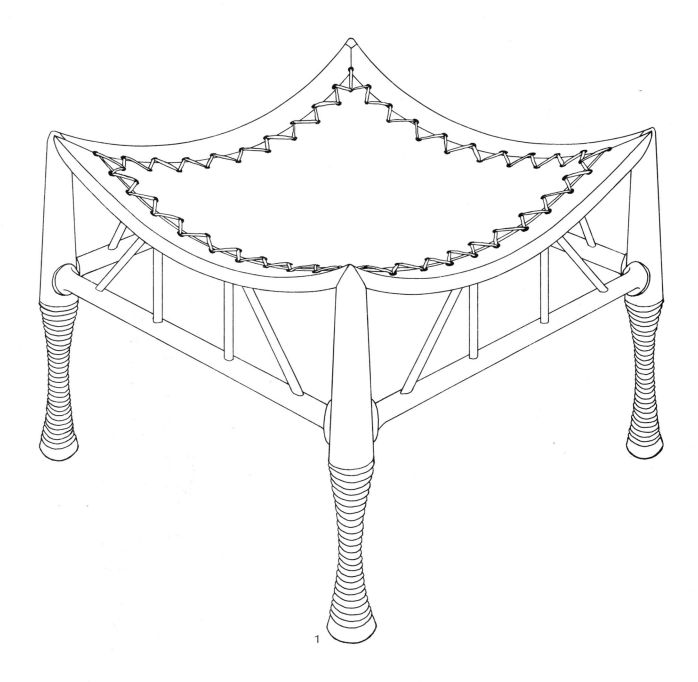

1

Liberty and Company

Liberty & Co. ranks with Samuel Bing's L'Art Nouveau and Julius Meier-Graefe's La Maison Moderne as one of the major commercial ventures to commission the work of turn of the century designers. The firm was highly successful, both in England and on the continent, and gave its name to the Italian style of Art Nouveau — 'Stile Liberty'.

Liberty & Co. was founded by Arthur Lasenby Liberty (1843-1917) when in 1875 he bought up the Japanese collection of his former employers Farmer and Rogers and established his own oriental retailers in Regent Street, London. The company expanded rapidly, and by the turn of the century was commissioning, importing and retailing fabrics, pottery, jewellery and silverware. Liberty's first furniture was commissioned in the early 1890s to supplement those pieces they imported from the East. At first the furniture was made in the Soho workshops of the French cabinet-maker Ursin Fortier, but in 1893 the company established its own furnishing and decorative studio under the direction of Leonard Wyburd.

Initially Liberty limited his output to furniture of Eastern inspiration and Tudor and Georgian imitations. By the turn of the century, however, he was commissioning designs from leading Arts and Crafts artists such as C. F. A. Voysey, George Walton and E. G. Punnett. Although Liberty catalogues insist that all the work was done by hand, in fact handwork was cut to a minimum and used only for finishing off and decoration, and Liberty's was thus able to make the work of the Arts and Crafts movement available to a far greater public. Designers remained anonymous, and their work was often altered to make it more in keeping with the 'Liberty Style' the firm sought to promote.

2

1   Thebes stool (1), 1884, walnut, mahogany or oak with turned legs and concave thonged leather seat. The Thebes stool, inspired by an ancient Egyptian model which also formed the basis of a chair by Holman Hunt (1885), was among the first products of Liberty's Furnishing and Decoration Studio. A second Thebes stool with three legs in solid oak or mahogany was also produced and was sold extensively in Europe, and stocked by Samuel Bing's L'Art Nouveau.
2   Reclining armchair, c.1905.
3   Bedroom of a London house furnished by Liberty's in 1897.
4   Chair and cabinet with glazed doors, part of a suite of satinwood furniture possibly to a design by George Walton, c.1901.

3

4

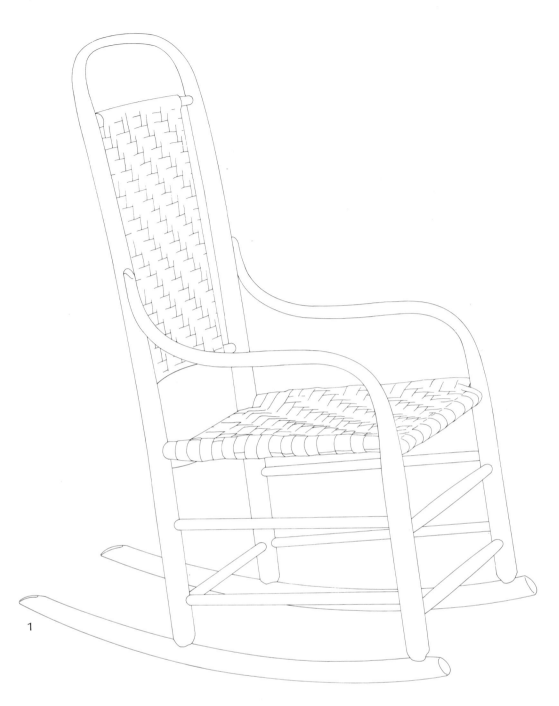

1

The Shakers

The Shaker sect was founded in England in 1747 and introduced to America in 1774 by Ann Lee (1736-1784). By 1825, nineteen independent Shaker communities had been established in New England, Kentucky, Ohio and Indiana. Their numbers gradually diminished towards the end of the nineteenth century, and only two communities survive today.

The Shakers consciously rejected the profane world to establish economically independent communities based on common ownership and the freedom and equality of all men and women. They attempted to produce everything they needed themselves, including the furniture for their own dwellings, and from 1852 furniture was manufactured in series and sold commercially as a source of income. Convinced that theirs was a more perfect world than the 'world outside', the Shakers strove for perfection in everything they did, and their beliefs that 'beauty is utility', 'anything may be called perfect which perfectly answers the purpose for which it is designed' and that any unnecessary frill or ornament was sinful led them to produce designs distinguished by a fitness for purpose and straightforward simplicity.

Although the first chairs produced in Shaker communities were indistinguishable from local production, the Shakers soon developed a distinctive style, and with the introduction of machine manufacture during the last quarter of the nineteenth century stereotyped methods and patterns developed. The first catalogues of their designs were published in 1874, and advertised three types of chair — upholstered, web-back (woven in fourteen colour variations) and slat-back — which could be produced with or without arms, cushions or rockers. Strength and durability were ensured by the use in the posts of carefully selected and seasoned hard maple, with the occasional use of cherry or birch, and much emphasis was placed on lightness, with the largest chair weighing just over ten pounds. The seats were usually cane, rush or plaited straw, and although most of the early chairs were painted dark red or stained with a thin red or yellow wash, the chairs of the late nineteenth century were stained to resemble

2

mahogany or old walnut, using commercially manufactured dyes. The Shakers were probably the first people in America to produce and use the rocking chair on a systematic scale.

1   Rocking chair with arms, bentwood with olive-coloured textile seat, after 1876. The U-shaped high back, curved arms and rockers were all made in one piece.
2   Maple armchair with green and pink plaited textile seat, New Lebanon c.1890.
3   *(from left to right)* Pinewood chair with plaited splint seat, New Lebanon c.1840; pinewood chair with plaited straw seat, Watervliet c.1875; maple child's chair with striped red and light brown textile seat, New Lebanon c.1890; dark stained oak chair with plaited ratan seat, Enfield c.1880.

3

1

Gustav Stickley

1857-1942

Gustav Stickley was the most influential disseminator of Arts and Crafts ideas in America, both through his own work and through his magazine *Craftsman,* founded in October 1901 to publicise the ideas of John Ruskin and William Morris, with contributions by leading American socialist writers. Stickley also used *Craftsman* to sell the output of his own firm, Craftsman Workshops, founded in 1898 after a visit to England where he was much impressed by the work of the Arts and Crafts movement. Craftsman Workshops expanded rapidly at the beginning of the twentieth century, acquiring a timber mill in the Adirondacks and opening a prestigious administrative office in New York City in 1905. By 1915, however, changing tastes led to a decline in

orders, and the bankrupt company was taken over by L. and J. G. Stickley as the Stickley Manufacturing Co., which still exists today.

In the catalogue to the Syracuse Arts and Crafts exhibition of 1903, Stickley outlined his aesthetic principles as 'the prominence of the structural idea, by which means an object frankly states the purpose for which it is intended. . . the absence of applied ornament, of all decoration that disguises or impairs the constructive features' and 'the strict fitting of all work to the medium in which it is executed'. His sturdy, simple chair designs, almost invariably in oak with rush or leather seats and without decoration, are a perfect embodiment of these ideals and

show the influence both of Morris and of Stickley's apprenticeship with his uncle, a cabinet-maker specialising in plain chairs with cane seats. Changes in taste and circumstances, however, forced Stickley to modify his principles, and from 1903-04 Harvey Ellis worked with him as a decorator, ornamenting furniture with inlaid metals and darker woods. By 1906, perhaps as a financial compromise after the opening of the New York office, he was championing the use of the machine in furniture production, although little attempt was made to change the designs or exploit the machine's advantages.

1   Reclining oak armchair made in the Craftsman Workshops c.1905.

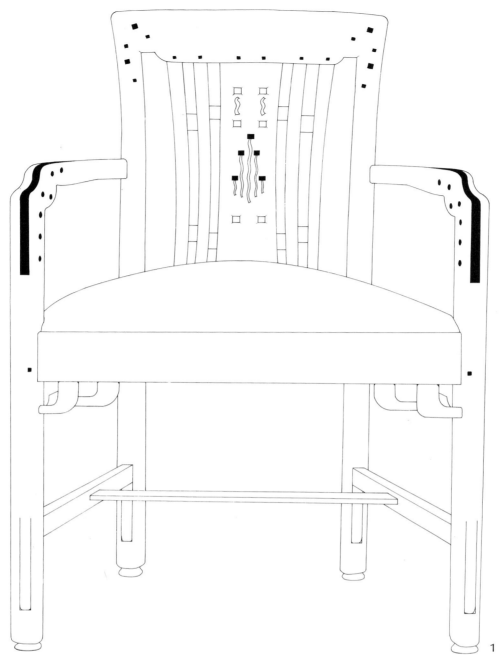

1

Greene,
Charles Sumner and
Henry Mather

1868-1957   1870-1954

The Greene brothers spent most of their working life in Southern California, where they developed a style of domestic architecture characterised by finely wrought craftsmanship and an appropriate use of natural materials. Their houses, which include the Bandini house (1903), the Ford and Blacker houses (1907), the Gamble house (1908) and the Pratt house (1909), represent the finest architectural expression of the Arts and Crafts movement in America, and were influenced both by their common interest in Japanese design and by Charles' knowledge of the English Arts and Crafts movement, gained during a visit to England in 1901.

The Greenes' early education was at Edward Woodward's St Louis Manual

Training High School, which was run on the principle that manual skills were a valuable and necessary part of education. They subsequently received a typical Beaux-Arts architectural training at the Massachusetts Institute of Technology, and worked in architectural offices in Boston before moving to Pasadena. Their best work was done during the first decade of the twentieth century, for their market was badly affected after the First World War by a new vogue for the Spanish Colonial style. Charles moved to Carmel in 1916 to concentrate on writing, while Henry continued to practise alone until the 1930s.

The Greenes' furniture was all commissioned by their clients, and was mostly designed by Charles, who believed that the

artist's noblest task was to make common materials beautiful for man. Their chairs were executed in wood, one of their favourite materials, which was hand rubbed with oil for several hours to enhance the natural grain. Although their early designs follow the work of Gustav Stickley, whose furniture they used in their first houses, they gradually established a style based on gently sculpted forms, with decorative elements emerging naturally from the construction. Their later work sometimes incorporated fine metal inlays and decorative panels carved with Japanese motifs.

The Greenes were much admired by the English Arts and Crafts practitioner Charles Ashbee, who visited their workshop

2

3

4

5

in 1909 and described their furniture as 'without exception the best and most characteristic I have seen in this country'.

1   Armchair designed for the Robert R. Blacker house, Hillcrest Avenue, Pasadena 1907.
2   Dining table and chairs from the David B. Gamble house, Westmoreland Place, Pasadena 1908.
3   Living room of the David B. Gamble house, with rocking chairs and side chair in polished wood with green upholstered seats.
4   Entrance hall, stairway and living room of the David B. Gamble house.
5   Mahogany chairs with leather seats and table designed for the Henry M. Robinson house, S. Grand Avenue, Pasadena 1905.
Opposite
1   GREENE AND GREENE Armchair designed in 1923 for the game room of the Mortimer Fleishhacker house, Albion Avenue, Woodside.
2   GREENE AND GREENE Armchair

designed for the living room of the Robert R. Blacker house, Hillcrest Avenue, Pasadena 1907.
3   MORRIS & CO. Saville armchair, designed by George Jack c.1890.
4   MORRIS & CO. Adjustable armchair, ebonised oak with velvet upholstery adapted by Philip Webb from a traditional design c.1865.
Overleaf
1   MACKMURDO Mahogany chair with carved and inlaid decoration, 1886.
2   MACKINTOSH Ebonised oak chair with upholstered seat, 1897.
3   OLBRICH Polished walnut chair with carved back, brass capped feet and upholstered seat, before 1900.
4   MOSER Armchair, beechwood stained dark and polished with upholstered seat and back and brass capped feet, 1901.

1

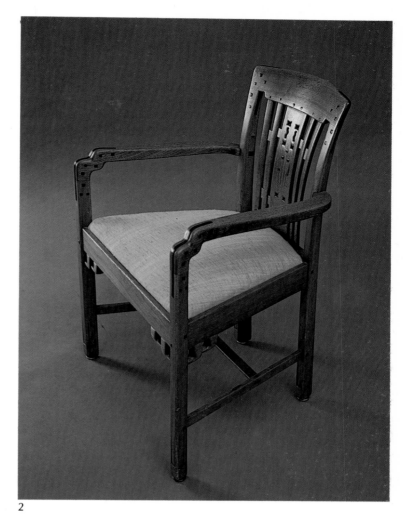

2

3

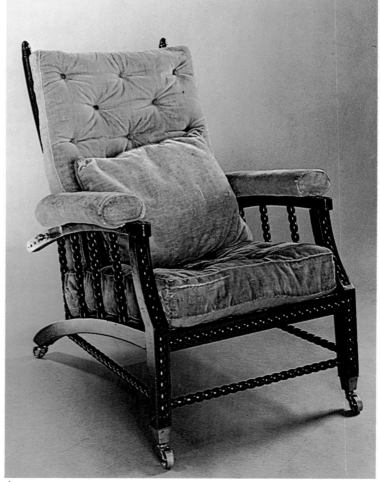

4

1

2

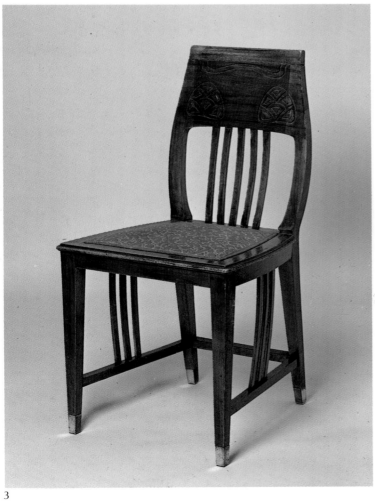

3

4

34

Art Nouveau

The turn of the century was the age of Art Nouveau, an extraordinary and exuberant international manifestation, the culmination of decades of theorising in a burst of novelty and innovation in the applied arts. Art Nouveau adopted a variety of stylistic guises, from the lush, organic styles that originated in France and Belgium to the cool refinement of the Glasgow or Austrian styles. Often quoted as one of the earliest precursors of Art Nouveau was a chair designed by Arthur Heygate Mackmurdo, founder of the Century Guild. His celebrated dining chair of 1882 is of traditional structure. The interest is in the fretwork back, a fluid, stylised interpretation of the lines of plant stems and, probably, the earliest example of the Art Nouveau emphasis on patterns of lines abstracted from nature. With few exceptions the English Art Nouveau chair was an insipid cross between the more rustic tendencies of the Arts and Crafts movement and the stylised plant themes of continental Art Nouveau. Liberty and Co. were once again foremost in the production of rather curious hybrids, often in mahogany and inlaid in pale woods or mother of pearl. Amongst the exceptions were the designs of architect/decorators Charles Francis Annesley Voysey, often very Arts and Crafts in feeling but occasionally aspiring to a refinement of line reminiscent of the Glasgow School, and M. H. Baillie Scott, similarly tied to the Arts and Crafts idea but responsible for attractive and unusual chairs, notably amongst a series of designs conceived for exhibit in Darmstadt. Here he has allowed full rein to a charming decorative style.

The most important name in the history of British chair design at the turn of the century was that of Charles Rennie Mackintosh, the Glasgow architect/designer. In a relatively brief career, enjoying only a limited, largely local, success between about 1895 and 1905, Mackintosh designed a remarkable range of chairs, always in the context of specific commissions and most often with a flagrant disregard for function. Mackintosh's chairs must be seen as items of sculpture to be looked at rather than sat upon, as intellectual or decorative exercises with a semi-religious character that was beautifully expressed by the contemporary critic Ahlers-Hestermann in his evocation of Mackintosh's interiors. 'Here', he said, 'indeed was the oddest mixture of puritanically severe forms designed for use, with a truly lyrical evaporation of all interest in usefulness. These rooms were like dreams, narrow panels, grey silk, very very slender wooden shafts - verticals everywhere. Little cupboards of rectangular shape . . . smooth, not of visible frame-and-panel construction; straight, white and serious-looking, as if they were young girls ready to go to their first holy communion - and yet not really; for somewhere there was a piece of decoration like a gem, never interfering with the contour, lines of hesitant elegance, like a faint, distant echo of van de Velde . . . Here was mysticism and asceticism, though by no means in a Christian sense, but with much of a scent of heliotrope, with well-manicured hands and a delicate sensuousness . . . As against the former overcrowding, there was hardly anything in these rooms, except that, say, two straight chairs, with backs as tall as a man, stood on a white carpet and looked silently and spectrally at each other across a little table.'

Mackintosh's architectural and design projects included the new Glasgow School of Art, the

MACKINTOSH White bedroom, Hill House, 1902.

WRIGHT Kaufmann office, 1937.

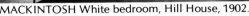

Queen's Cross Church, Scotland Street School and, most significantly from the point of view of his chair design, a series of tea-rooms in Glasgow for his most enlightened patron, Miss Cranston, and a small number of private houses, including the magnificent Hill House, Helensburgh of 1902. His first high-back chair, and, perhaps, today, his best known, was the dark-stained oak chair with the oval head-rest above two flat splats which he created in 1897 for the Argyle Street tea-rooms, and which he used subsequently in other schemes, including exhibitions and his own home. The fretted motif in the oval is a highly stylised swallow in flight, an almost complete abstraction and a fascinating progression from the more naturalistic interpretation of the same subject in a sketch of 1893-4. Certain sturdy designs in natural oak reflect the Scottish baronial tradition behind Mackintosh's work, but he is at his most exciting working in slender shafts of ebonised wood in designs exploiting subtly balanced interplays of horizontal and vertical lines, and in the sophisticated white-painted high-backs designed for Miss Cranston or for foreign exhibition projects. Most extraordinary amongst the ebonised wood designs are the curved lattice-back chair designed for the Willow tea-rooms in 1904 and the delicate, feather-light ladderback of 1902 for the white bedroom at Hill House, these latter somehow providing a conceptual link between the linear sophistication of Japanese art and the emergent ideology of skyscraper architecture. From 1902 also dates Mackintosh's project for the Wärndorfer Musik Salon in Vienna, a project which included a beautiful white high-back chair with carved detail picked out in mauve and with distinctive stylised roses stencilled on the upholstered back. Two years later, for the room de luxe in Miss Cranston's Willow tea-rooms, he created another elegant white high-back, upholstered in mauve silk-velvet and this time with a strictly geometric chequer-pattern motif picked out in silver. Mackintosh was an original, without precursors and, aside from a relatively short-lived period of mutual admiration with a group of artists in Vienna, without any real following outside Glasgow.

In the United States Frank Lloyd Wright showed affinities with Mackintosh's architectural approach to chair design, creating elegant chairs which exploited similarly exaggerated verticals. A set of dining chairs designed in 1908 for Frederick C. Robie of Chicago are particularly successful with their tall backs of angular vertical splats.

Mackintosh's ideas were warmly received in Vienna by the group of artists led by Josef Hoffmann and including Koloman Moser, Otto Wagner and Joseph Maria Olbrich who had styled themselves as the Vienna Secessionists before forming the Wiener Werkstätte in 1903 to put into practice their new attitudes to design. The uncluttered sophistication of Mackintosh's work had an immediate impact on their collective style and strict geometry and chequer patterns dominated the group's work in the years following their initial exposure to Mackintosh in 1900. Koloman Moser designed a set of dining chairs in 1904 which clearly show this debt yet have a distinctly Austrian character. The strict lines are relieved by the rich figured wood and a mother of pearl and wood inlay of a stylised bird adds a note of luxury to the austere flat backs. The hammered metal sabots

WAGNER Armchair, 1902.   OLBRICH Side chair, 1899.   HOFFMANN Armchair, 1905.   THONET Armchair, c.1851.

are a characteristically Viennese touch. A favourite feature of Hoffmann's designs were the wooden spheres that emphasised joints; he also showed a predilection for the circular section structural member and devised new designs for manufacture in the bentwood that had first been popularised many decades earlier by Michael Thonet.

Thonet chairs in bentwood and cane escape easy categorisation. First conceived in the 1830s, certain designs are still in production today and fit as easily into modern settings as they did into contemporary interiors. Michael Thonet set up a furniture factory in 1819 at Boppard in Germany and worked for some ten years in pursuit of an ideal means of making light wooden furniture of a design suitable for mass-production. He found the answer in turned bentwood, exhibiting his first chair design in this material in 1830. The firm was dissolved in 1842 and Thonet took up an invitation to design furniture for the Austrian Royal Household in Vienna. By 1849 he felt ready to set up a factory once again, this time in Vienna. In 1853 his five sons joined his enterprise which by the time of Thonet's death in 1871 was the largest furniture factory in the world. Two of his best known designs, his rocking chair and 'Viennese' chair, were designed in 1850. The latter was a prize winner when exhibited in London in 1851 and, to date, over fifty million of this design have been sold. Hoffmann, Wagner and Loos contributed designs to the Thonet factory and during the twenties the firm manufactured the designs of another generation including Marcel Breuer, Le Corbusier, Mies van der Rohe and Mart Stam.

Around 1900 German chair design, more organic in feeling than its Austrian counterpart, gave no hint of the revolution to come in the 1920s. 'Jugendstil', as German Art Nouveau was known, prevailed. The style developed in two particular centres - Munich, where the nucleus that emerged around 1895 included Otto Eckmann, Hermann Obrist, August Endell, Bernhard Pankok and Richard Riemerschmid, and Darmstadt, in the artists' colony set up by the Grand Duke Ernst Ludwig of Hesse under Joseph Maria Olbrich, brought in from Vienna. The Munich style chair aimed at an organic design but without the luxurious indulgence of detail characteristic of contemporary French work. One is reminded more of skeleton-like joints than elegant plant forms, particularly in certain chairs by Endell and Obrist which have curious knobbly organic joints. Riemerschmid designed an elegant chair in 1899 with sweeping lines curving diagonally from back-rest to front feet. The design was retailed in London by Liberty & Co. The Darmstadt designer Hans Christiansen created a notably stylish box armchair exploiting angularity with lightness and sophistication, more evocative perhaps of Austrian than of German taste.

Chair design during the Art Nouveau period found its most organic expression in France where design and decorative innovation emanated from two distinct centres, Paris and the provincial town of Nancy where Emile Gallé had influenced a whole generation of artisans. The Paris style was more sophisticated, at least in the more superficial points. A Paris Art Nouveau chair would be of lighter construction than its provincial counterpart, less naturalistic, playing with more highly

GUIMARD Hôtel Guimard, 1909-12.   MAJORELLE Café de Paris, 1899.   VAN DE VELDE Dining-room, c.1899.

refined patterns of abstract lines and forms. The greatest exponent of this Paris interpretation was the architect/designer Hector Guimard, at the height of his success during the 1890s and early 1900s. Guimard's chair designs are exercises in a totally personal abstract-organic style of sculpture. His working drawings could not be diagrammatic, like an architect's plans, but were drawn in tones to render the subtle detail which his craftsmen were to interpret. It is easy to overlook the fact that Guimard's chairs are carved in wood, such is the fluid freedom of their design. Whilst his early creations, in a variety of woods, are more eccentric in form, including an extraordinary banquette of 1897-8 drawn in manic whiplashes, his later chairs, usually in pearwood, display a more mellow interpretation of the organic. Other exponents of the Paris style include, notably, Edward Colonna and Eugène Gaillard, who created fully modelled maquettes for his sculptural chairs, and Georges de Feure, who designed seat furniture in pale or gilt wood, upholstered in embroidered silk.

In Nancy Emile Gallé designed a number of chairs, the most interesting of which is undoubtedly his dining chair 'aux ombelles', the back-rest carved in the shape of a stylised spray of cow parsley in the manner of a *tsuba* or Japanese sword guard. More interesting are those chairs made by the group of local furniture makers who came under Gallé's influence. Most significant in the range and variety of his production was Louis Majorelle. At his most inventive he created dynamic designs, carved in mahogany or oak, exploiting the rhythmic interplay of interflowing organically carved limbs. The mahogany would on occasion be ornamented with gilt bronze sabots and details sensuously modelled on plant themes. Eugène Vallin and Jacques Gruber created chairs in a similar vein though with a tendency to heaviness.

In other European countries, in Belgium, Italy, and Spain, the Art Nouveau movement found colourful and distinctive practitioners, each adding a new facet to the history of chair design. Belgian Art Nouveau was a blend of Arts and Crafts idealism and the French taste for luxury. The style adopted was essentially organic, but in a less decadent, less indulgent vein than that favoured in France. The Belgian style has a powerful graphic dynamism and found its strongest expression in the designs of Victor Horta and Henry van de Velde. Horta's chairs are constructed of emphatic lines conveying a sense of organic growth but generally without recourse to carved detailing. Van de Velde's was a slightly more austere version of the same style. Gustave Serrurier-Bovy also produced noteworthy seat furniture and would often give a design a plural function. A banquette, for example, might be surmounted by vitrines, two armchairs joined by shelving. Here were the beginnings of 'unit' furniture.

In Italy, in his Milan workshops, the eccentric Carlo Bugatti evolved unique chair designs reaching an apogee in his projects for the Turin exhibition of 1902. It was in the 1880s that he embarked on the production of furniture, which included remarkable asymmetrical chairs in inlaid ebony, beaten copper and painted vellum in quasi-Arab taste with elements of Japonaiserie.

LOUIS XVI style chairs, c.1900.

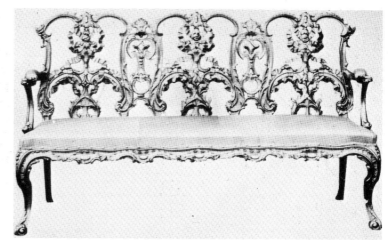

CHIPPENDALE style settee, c.1900.

During the 1890s vellum came to play a more important part and his inlays acquired a light, abstract discipline. The public was hardly prepared, however, for the shock of the remarkable furniture shown in Turin. Purely sculptural exercises, his 1902 chairs were completely covered in finely decorated vellum, disguising the wood substructure and emphasising the fluid freedom of his novel shapes.

In Spain, in Barcelona, another eccentric, the architect Antonio Gaudí, devised his own Baroque version of the Art Nouveau chair, not dissimilar in its somewhat uncomfortable-looking interpretation of the organic, to the products of the Munich group, but more personal, more exaggerated and experimenting with the combined use of carved wood and wrought metal.

The Art Nouveau movement brought forth a veritable tidal wave of chair designs and the importance placed upon so many of these by historians could easily lead to the impression that every smart home at the turn of the century was furnished by designers such as Guimard or Gaudí, Horta or Hoffmann. It is perhaps time to redress the balance by emphasising the continuing popularity with a very broad public of revivalist, conservative styles. The avant-garde designs were for an appreciative minority and, indeed, in so many instances were created for specific commissions and destined for limited contemporary exposure. Not until chair designers applied themselves seriously to design for mass-production could the avant-garde chair be anything but élitist. Thonet was an isolated exception to the general pattern. Nor should one overlook the traditional conservatism of inherited wealth or indeed the equally traditional desire for conspicuous opulence of the nouveaux riches. During the last quarter of the nineteenth century, for example, the new wealthy families of East Coast America were pandered to by expensive decorators with furniture in a rich neo-Byzantine style which became sanctioned as 'official' taste in such projects as Henry Hobson Richardson's contribution to the furbishing of the State Capitol.

In England the turn of the century and the Edwardian period saw a strong revival of eighteenth-century chair designs, differentiated from the originals by a tendency to a thinner construction. Sheraton and Hepplewhite style chairs found a ready market. When the chic new Ritz hotel was opened in 1904, guests entered a foyer filled with Louis XVI style chairs and tea tables. In France, where the strongly archaeological Second Empire style had enjoyed such popularity, revivalism was a strong element and traditions refused to be ousted by novelty. It is typical that the society portraitists Boldini and Helleu should consistently depict their society lady subjects on eighteenth-century style chairs.

Nor was this a pattern to be easily changed during the twentieth century. When in his study *L'Art Décoratif d'Aujourd'hui,* published in 1925, Le Corbusier holds up for criticism the industry of manufacturing fake eighteenth-century chairs one is tempted to observe that although Le Corbusier may have enjoyed a greater *succès de scandale* for his bold innovations, it was the purveyors of revivalist styles who enjoyed lasting commercial success.

1

Arthur Heygate Mackmurdo

1851-1942

English architect and decorative designer, Mackmurdo received a conventional architectural training in the offices of T. Chatfield Clarke and James Brooks before setting up his own architectural practice in London in 1875. He was much influenced by John Ruskin, whose lectures he attended in 1873, and by the architecture of the Italian Renaissance, which he studied when accompanying Ruskin to Italy the following year. Apart from Ruskin's St George's Guild, the Century Guild, founded in 1882 by Mackmurdo and Selwyn Image, was the first British craft guild, and was thus highly influential in shaping the Arts and Crafts movement. Formed with the aim of 'rendering all branches of art the sphere no

longer of the tradesman but of the artist', the Century Guild included sculptors, metalworkers, enamellists and stained-glass designers among its members and carried out decorative work of all kinds. The Guild received few commissions after 1888, and Mackmurdo concentrated on architecture, which he renounced in 1904 to develop his currency reform theories.

Because of the cooperative policy of the Century Guild it is difficult to attribute designs with certainty, although it is probable that most of the furniture used in the Guild's decorative schemes between 1882 and 1888 was designed by Mackmurdo. All the Century Guild's pieces were made by established cabinet-makers, including Collinson & Lock and Goodall &

Co. of Manchester and Wilkinson & Son of Old Bond Street.

Mackmurdo's chair designs are a curious combination of original form and classical details such as the projecting cornices on the music room settle exhibited at the Inventions Exhibition of 1885 and on the chair designed for the Century Guild Stand at the Liverpool International Exhibition of 1886. Mostly in satinwood or mahogany with decorative inlay, Mackmurdo's pieces are dependent for their effect on balance, proportion and strongly contrasting verticals and horizontals. The carved back of his dining chair of 1882-83, with its formalised organic decoration, is often quoted as the earliest manifestation of the Art Nouveau style.

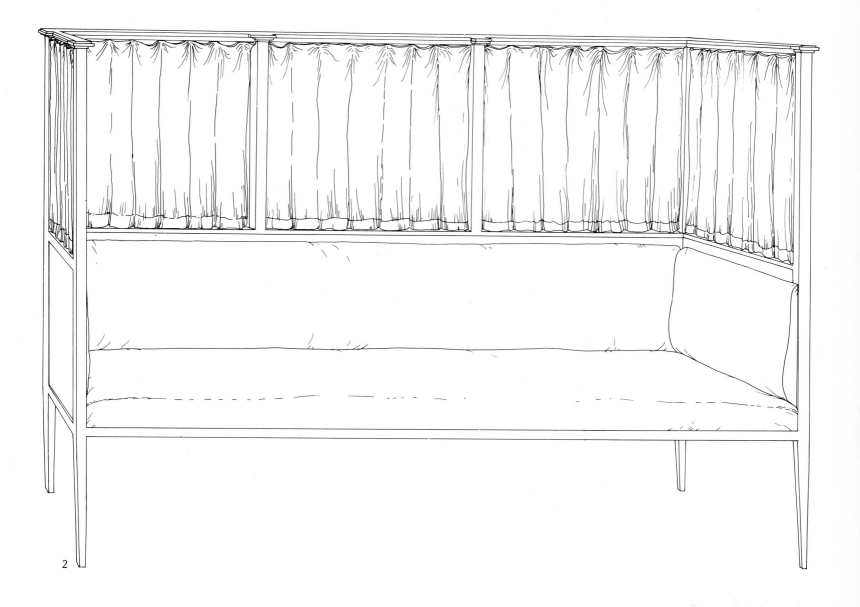

2

1   Mahogany dining chair with upholstered
seat designed for the Century Guild and
manufactured by Collinson & Lock c.1882-83.
The elaborate fretwork back with painted
decoration represents one of the earliest
manifestations of the Art Nouveau style.
2   Mahogany settle with projecting cornice
and chintz curtains designed for the Century
Guild and manufactured by Wilkinson & Son
of Old Bond Street, c.1888.
3   Mahogany settle with cane insets and
hangings, upholstery and cushions in the Morris
'Tulip' chintz c.1886.

3

1

Charles Francis Annesley Voysey

1857-1941

1 Chair for the Essex and Suffolk Equitable Insurance Company, oak with embossed leather seat and back, c.1907.
2 Dining chair with arms, oak with leather upholstered seat, c.1902.

Charles Francis Annesley Voysey was one of the most influential pioneers of British domestic architecture, and it was through him that the principles of the English Arts and Crafts movement found their most perfect architectural expression. His characteristic style based on simplicity, good proportion and fitness for purpose was widely copied, and established him as a major influence in the development of the English suburban house.

Voysey trained in the architectural offices of J. P. Seddon, Saxon Snell and George Devey before setting up his own practice in 1882. Although at first he concentrated on textile and wallpaper designs inspired by Arthur Heygate Mackmurdo, from the time of his first architectural commission in 1888 until the outbreak of the First World War he was to build over fifty country houses throughout England, including the Grey House, Bedford Park (1891), Perrycroft, Herefordshire (1893), Broadleys, Lancashire (1898) and his own house, The Orchard, Chorley Wood (1900). As well as these domestic commissions, for which he often designed every detail of the interior including furniture, decoration, carpets and curtains, Voysey also built offices and a factory in London. He received the awards of Designer for Industry from the Royal Society of Arts (1936) and Gold Medal from the RIBA at the end of his lifetime.

Like his architecture, Voysey's furniture is characterised by its simplicity, with an emphasis on careful design and good proportion. His chairs were designed specifically to meet the needs of everyday domestic life and are essentially English in character. Unlike many of his contemporaries, Voysey was prepared to use the machine to his own advantage, working within the 'limited vocabulary' it imposed. Between 1895 and 1910 he established a style based on the production of a limited range of designs usually in untreated oak, which he adapted and modified to various uses. Occasional atypical pieces include the bedroom chair of 1896 or the tub chair of 1902. Voysey's work was manufactured by a small number of craft firms including F. C. Nielsen, Thallen and A. W. Simpson.

2

3   Interior of the house of Mrs Van Gruisen, Birkenhead, remodelled by Voysey in 1904.
4   Interior of the house of E. J. Horniman, Garden Corner, Chelsea Embankment, remodelled by Voysey in 1906-07.

3

4

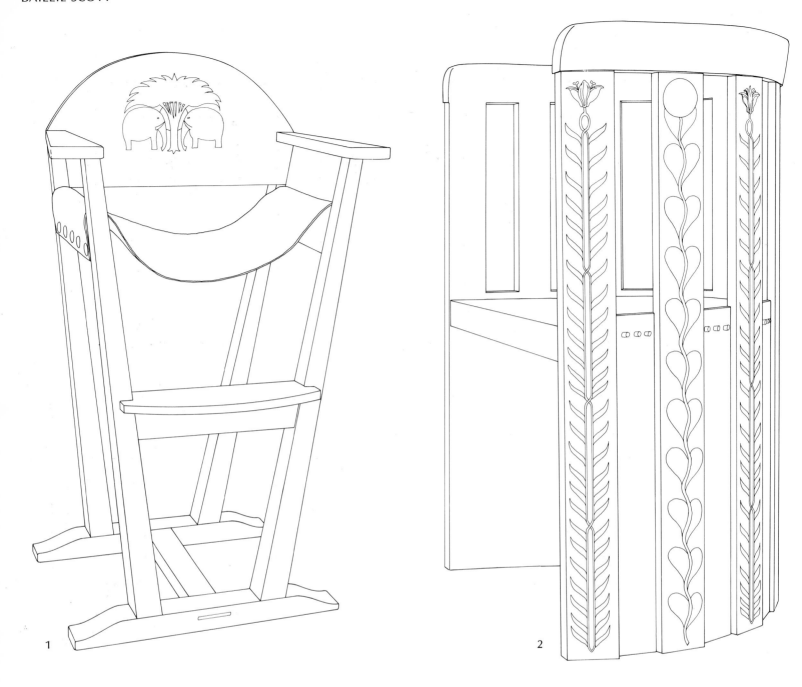

1

2

Mackay Hugh Baillie Scott

1865-1945

English architect and designer, Mackay Hugh Baillie Scott abandoned his training in agriculture in 1886 and was articled to Charles Davis, City Architect of Bath. Three years later he moved to the Isle of Man where he worked initially for the architect F. Sanderson, attending classes at the School of Art in his spare time. From the establishment of his own architectural office in the Isle of Man in 1893 until his retirement in 1939, Baillie Scott practised in Bedford, Bath and finally London, although the majority of his work was carried out between 1893 and 1910. His realisation of the possibilities of the small country house, influenced by the work of C. F. A. Voysey, brought him widespread publicity both at home and abroad, with over 200 com-

missions for houses, cottages and interior schemes. A collection of his articles and projects was published as *Houses and Gardens* in 1906.

Baillie Scott believed that furniture 'should appear to grow out of the requirements of the room... and not as an alien importation from the upholsterer', and most of his furniture was designed for his own houses. Like most Arts and Crafts designers, he distinguished between everyday furniture and show piece items, and his chair designs include simple pieces such as the rush-bottomed chair of 1897 or the high-backed armchair covered in floral fabric of 1906, as well as more elaborate items such as the semi-circular writing chair designed for the Ducal Palace in

3

4

Darmstadt. His chairs are characterised by a careful study of proportion and are of simple design ornamented with colour and relief. Flat surfaces are often inlaid with coloured woods, ivory or pewter in stylised natural forms 'to suggest and reflect in however small degree some of the beauty of the earth'.

Baillie Scott's furniture was manufactured and retailed by J. P. White of Bedford who in 1902 advertised *A Book of Furniture* by Baillie Scott containing over one hundred items. Like his architecture, his furniture received much publicity abroad, and in 1903 an issue of *Zeitschrift für Innendekoration* was devoted exclusively to his designs.

1   Child's chair, oak inlaid with coloured woods. The chair was manufactured and retailed by J. P. White of Bedford, and featured in the 1902 catalogue of Baillie Scott's designs.
2   Semi-circular writing chair, carved oak with applied ornament, designed for the Grand Duke of Hesse's palace in Darmstadt in 1897 and made by C. R. Ashbee's Guild of Handicraft. The inspiration for this design was a chair which appeared in one of Edward Burne-Jones' tapestries for William Morris.
3   Armchair, oak with embossed leather back, designed for the Grand Duke of Hesse in 1897 and made by the Guild of Handicraft.
4   Oak settle inlaid with pewter and ebonised fruitwood, 1901. Manufactured by J. P. White of Bedford, and advertised as 'No. 2 Settle', with a retail price of £12.
5   Oak chair with leather seat, c.1901.

5

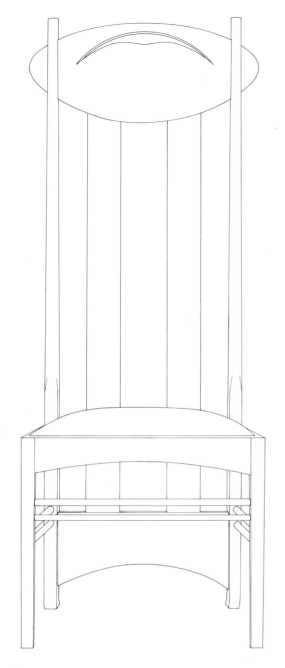

1

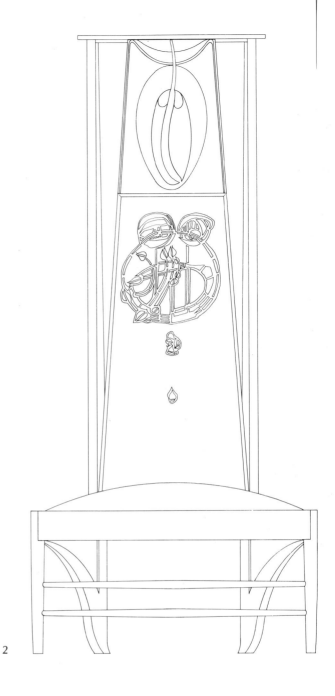

2

Charles Rennie Mackintosh

1868-1928

Charles Rennie Mackintosh was one of the truly original creative talents of the generation of architects whose careers spanned the turn of the century. Although his architectural output is meagre — fourteen completed buildings and several interiors — his work is widely acknowledged as important in the development of Modern architecture.

Mackintosh trained at the Glasgow School of Art from 1885 to 1892, and then worked as an apprentice to the architect John Hutchison before joining the practice of Honeyman and Keppie in 1889. The spirit of his work is encapsulated in his major achievement, the Glasgow School of Art, and in this building alone can be seen the development of his career from the

Scottish Baronial and Art Nouveau influences of the original building of 1897-99 to the geometric, Modernist purism of the extension of 1907-09.

As well as his architectural work, Mackintosh also collaborated in the design of posters and other graphic works with 'The Four' — a group whose other members were the sisters Frances and Margaret Macdonald and Herbert MacNair. He resigned his architectural partnership in 1913, and in 1920 moved to Port de Vendres, France, where he devoted himself to watercolour painting.

Mackintosh's chair designs are totally devoid of historical precedent and as such represent the most innovative and individual British furniture of the period.

Each piece was designed to enhance the consciously created atmosphere of a specific setting, and to solve the 'artistic' problem of filling interior space in the most pleasing manner possible.

Mackintosh's most characteristic designs are the high-backed chairs, whose attenuated lines are reflected in the graphic work of 'The Four' which earned them the nickname of the 'Spook School'. Mackintosh designed several variations of the high-backed chair in dark stained oak, including one with two vertical slats, an oval top and horse-hair seat for Miss Cranston's Argyle Street tea-rooms (1897), a design with a fabric seat and two vertical slats decorated with a characteristic geometrical arrangement of rectangular cut-

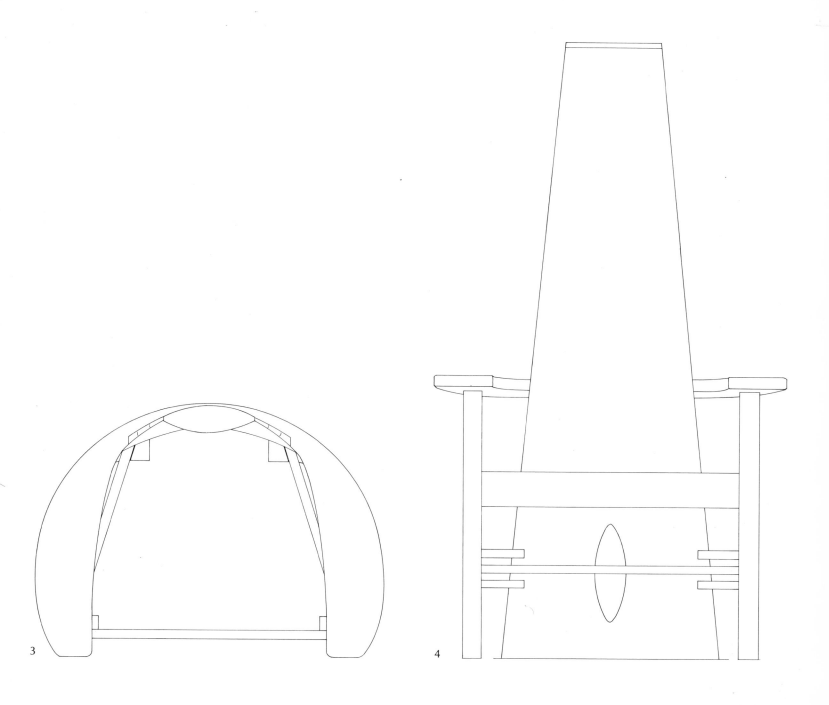

3

4

outs for the Ingram Street tea-rooms (1900) with companion medium and low-backed versions, a chair with a solid tapering back for the front hall of Windyhill (1900), and the famous ladderback for the bedroom of Hill House (1902).

As his interiors often relied on a dramatic contrast of black and white, Mackintosh also designed several white chairs with an enamel-like surface obtained by a coach-painting technique. These include the chair for his own Mains Street flat (1900), which was a white version of the Ingram Street chair with rectangular glass insets, and the chairs for the Turin exhibition of 1902. The stencilled decoration of the latter is a characteristic Mackintosh motif based on a full-blown

rose — a design which was later developed by Paul Iribe to become one of the key motifs of Art Deco.

As well as his high-backed chairs Mackintosh also produced less dramatic designs, characterised by unusual backs made up of a geometrical arrangement of squares and rectangles as well as more sturdy, Arts and Crafts type chairs such as the armchairs for the board room of the Glasgow School of Art (1899) or the low-backed armchair for his own Mains Street flat (1900). Unlike his English contemporaries, his major preoccupation was the visual appeal of his designs, and his chairs, especially the high-backed series, are often criticised for their lack of comfort and practicality.

1   Ebonised oak chair with upholstered horse-hair seat chequered in black and blue, designed in 1897 for the central tables of Miss Cranston's Argyle Street tea-rooms and exhibited at the Vienna Secession in 1900. This was the first of Mackintosh's high-backed designs, and unusual in the oval headrest with its stylised swallow motif.
2   High-backed chair, oak painted white with linen upholstery, exhibited in the Rose boudoir at the Turin exhibition of 1902. The stencilled decoration in pink and green and head rest, with purple glass insets, use a characteristic Mackintosh motif based on the rose. A companion medium-backed chair with arms using the same motif was also exhibited at Turin and at Moscow the following year.
3, 4 Stained oak armchair with tapering back and rush seat, designed for the hallway of Windyhill, Kilmalcolm, in 1901.

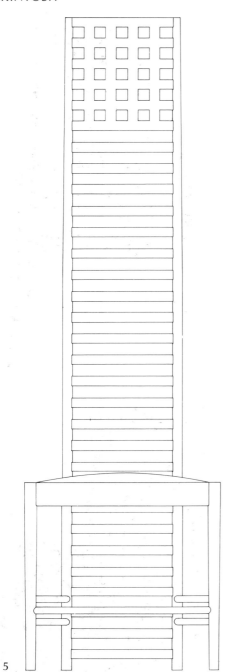

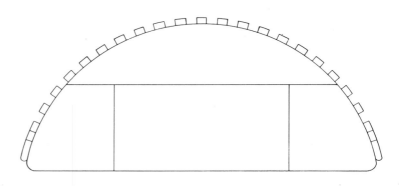

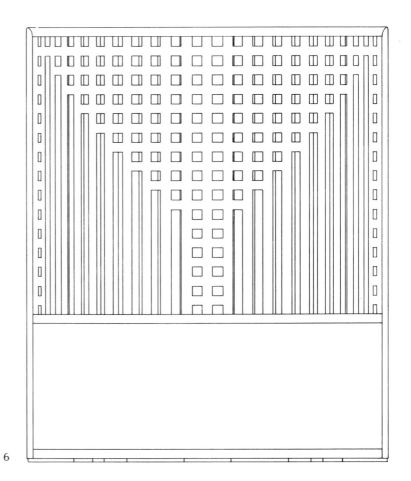

5

6

5   Ladderback chair, ebonised oak with upholstered seat, designed for the bedroom of Hill House, Helensburgh, in 1903.
6   Curved lattice back chair in stained oak designed in 1904 for the order desk of Miss Cranston's Willow Street tea-rooms.
7   The Back Saloon in Miss Cranston's Willow Street tea-rooms, in 1903.
8   Guest bedroom, 78 Derngate, Northampton 1919. The chairs are in light oak with a Secession-style blue and black chequer border.

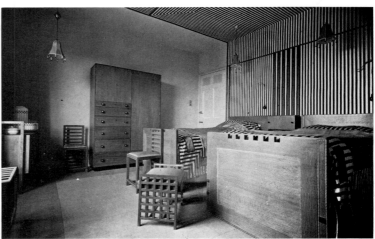

7

8

2

3

1

George Walton

1867-1933

A Scottish architect and interior decorator, George Walton was one of a number of architects and designers working in Glasgow at the turn of the century, and collaborated with Charles Rennie Mackintosh in the decoration of Miss Cranston's Buchanan Street tea-rooms in 1896. Although his only artistic training was through evening classes at the Glasgow School of Art, Walton was nevertheless able to open his own interior decorating business — George Walton and Co., Ecclesiastical and House Decorators — in 1888, which was soon extended to include a workshop. In 1897 Walton moved to London, and by 1898 he owned workshops in London and York. The turning point in his career, however, came when he met George Davison, head of Kodak European sales who, between 1897 and 1902, commissioned him to design shop fronts, interiors and furnishings for Kodak branches in Brussels, Glasgow, Milan, Vienna, Moscow and London. Walton's architectural work consisted mainly of private country houses, including The Leys, Elstree and The White House, Shiplake. He worked as architect and designer for the Central Liquor Traffic Control Board from 1916 to 1921, after which he carried out only a few minor commissions.

Walton's chair designs were usually executed in oak, either stained to give a darker tone or painted white, with cane, rush or upholstered seats and carved backs, often using his favourite motif of a cut-out heart. Sturdy yet stylish, they reduce the attenuated exaggerations of the Glasgow School to a more practical elegance, as can be seen in his chairs for the smoking room of the Buchanan Street tea-rooms. His furniture was manufactured by his own firm, Liberty's and various High Wycombe cabinet-makers.

1   Stained oak armchair with rush seat, adapted from a traditional Scottish model and used in Miss Cranston's Buchanan Street tea-rooms in 1896 and in several European Kodak showrooms.
2   Ebonised oak armchair, c.1896.
3   Walnut armchair with inlaid decoration, c.1899. Manufactured by William Birch of High Wycombe and sold as a drawing-room chair by Liberty & Co.

1   Oak side chair designed for the Isabel Roberts house, River Forest, Illinois, 1908.
2   Oak side chair with dark brown stain finish designed for the Francis W. Little house, Wayzata, Minnesota, 1913.
3   Painted steel and walnut chair with upholstered seat and back designed for the Johnson Wax Building, 1936-39.
4   Side chair in Philippine mahogany, designed for the house of Wright's son David, Phoenix, Arizona 1952.
5   Dining chair, redwood with upholstered cushion, designed for the house of Dr and Mrs Paul Hanna, Palo Alto, California 1936.
6   Oak chair designed for the Dana house, Springfield, Illinois 1903.
7   Oak armchair designed for the Ray W. Evans house, Beverly Hills, Illinois 1908.
8   Oak armchair designed for the Darwin D. Martin house, Buffalo 1904.

Frank Lloyd Wright

1867-1959

In the course of a career which spanned the periods of Art Nouveau and the Modern Movement, Frank Lloyd Wright produced over three hundred houses and several larger commissions which established him as the greatest American architect of the twentieth century.

Wright's first known experiment in designing and executing a total environment was the dining-room of his own house (1895) in which the vertical emphasis of the high-backed chairs contrasted with the horizontal emphasis of the panelling of the room. These chairs and the 'cube' chair of the same year established a style based on rigid geometrical forms and refined proportions, devoid of ornament, which was to characterise the rest of his work.

Their Japanese-inspired vertical slats were to become a feature of subsequent dining chairs such as those for the Husser house (1899) and Robie house (1908).

Wright's conception of organic architecture required that all the furnishings in his buildings express the spirit of the whole, an approach which was taken to extremes in the chairs designed for the Hollyhock house (1920), whose backs are formed of the same stylised hollyhock motif used on the concrete facade, or those of the David Wright house (1952), in which the circular seats were intended as a reflection of the house's circular plan.

Although Wright produced designs for metal chairs, including the painted steel chairs with oak seats for the Larkin building

(1904), and the lighter steel and walnut chairs with upholstered seats and backs for the Johnson Wax building (1936-39), his favoured material was wood, especially 'quartered' oak, which gave the most attractive grain. He continued to design furniture throughout his career, including inexpensive, easily manufactured chairs for the 'Usonian' houses of the late 1930s, and chairs for the luxury houses of the 1940s and 1950s.

Overleaf
1   MACKINTOSH Glasgow School of Art board room, 1899.
2   WRIGHT Dining room of his own house, Oak Park, 1895. The chairs were remodelled c.1900.

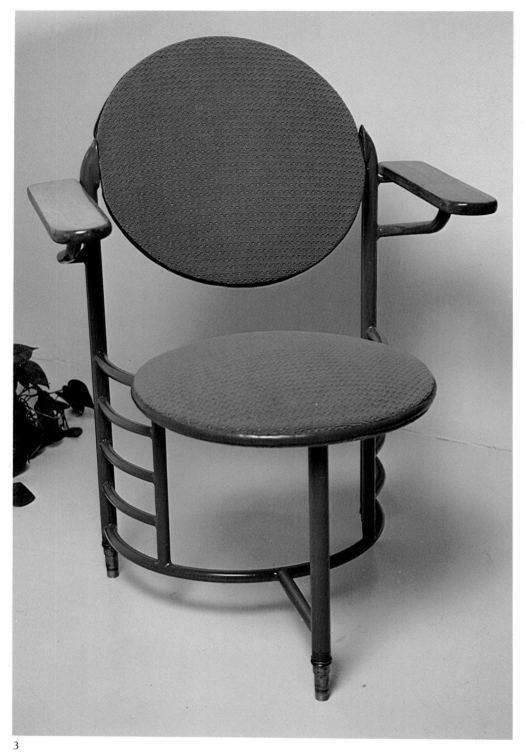

3

4

5

6

7

8

1

2

Previous Page
MOSER Armchair, 1904, amboyna veneer, upholstered seat and back and a characteristic Secession border made up of small pale wood squares. The beak and wings of the stylised bird in the centre of the back are in mother-of-pearl.

Opposite
HOFFMANN Beechwood armchair with leather seat, designed in 1905 for the Cabaret Fledermaus, Vienna and manufactured by Kohn & Kohn.

1   Chair no. 14, 1859.
2   One of the simplest of Thonet's chairs, designed in 1885.
3   Chair no. 51, c.1870-80.
4   Reclining chaise-longue, no. 9702, with adjustable back which also folds over the seat for easier storage.
5   Chair no. 9, c. 1870. One of Thonet Brothers' most popular designs, the chair no. 9 was used frequently by Le Corbusier in his interiors of the 1920s.

1   2   3

4

Thonet Brothers

Thonet Brothers was established in 1819 at Boppard by Michael Thonet (1796-1871), although experiments with the turned bentwood for which the firm became known did not begin until 1830. This first venture was financially unsuccessful, and in 1842 Thonet moved to Vienna where he worked for Carl Leistler. After several successful commissions from the wealthy Viennese court for his classical bentwood furniture, including that for the Liechtenstein Palace (1843-46), Thonet was able to establish his own workshop in 1849 with the help of his five sons. Seven years later he opened a factory in Koritschan, Moravia, designing the building and much of the machinery himself. At Koritschan he was able to take advantage of cheap rural labour and wood from the surrounding red-beech forests — a material which was later to become central to the production of bentwood furniture. The company's first patents expired in 1869, opening the market for competitors, and in 1871 Michael Thonet died. The firm continued under the direction of his sons, and by 1876 was employing 4,500 workers and mass-producing 2,000 pieces of bentwood furniture a day, 1,750 of which were chairs. By 1900, the daily production of the factory's 26 branches had risen to 15,000 pieces, and Thonet catalogues from the turn of the century illustrate chairs of every imaginable kind, including an office range, armchairs and settees and scaled-down versions for children. Thonet Brothers

5

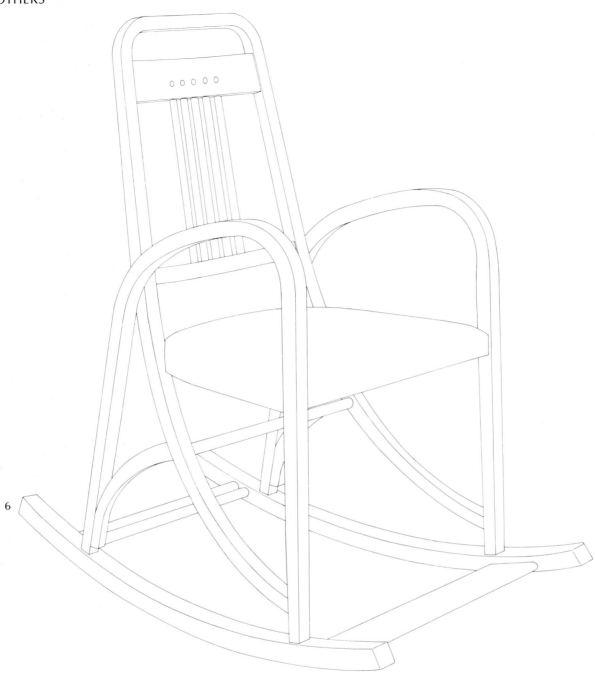

6

maintained a pioneering spirit, manufacturing chairs by Otto Wagner, Adolf Loos and Josef Hoffmann and subsequently producing the tubular steel designs of Mart Stam, Marcel Breuer, Mies van der Rohe and Le Corbusier. The firm is still in existence, and is at present directed by a member of the Thonet family.

Thonet's chairs were unique in their combination of beauty of form, inexpensiveness and versatility, and alone among his contemporaries he succeeded in designing elegant, well-made furniture suitable for mass-production and cheap enough to be accessible to the public at large. The bentwood technique, which was gradually improved from his first experiments in the 1830s, involved cutting the

wood into laths which were steamed to attain flexibility, then clamping the steamed laths to iron strips which were bent in such a way that all the fibres of the wood were forced to compress, producing a structurally rigid form. Technical improvement allowed a simplification of form and reduction in the thickness of parts, and by 1860 machinery was used to bring the wood into its final shape. As Thonet expanded, new techniques were developed — for example the idea of using bolts rather than glue to join the pieces together arose in answer to the problem of catering for the humid South American climate.

The most classic Thonet design was the chair no. 14, which sold over 50 million

between its conception in 1859 and 1930. The chair, sold in kit form and assembled at its destination, represented the culmination of Thonet's search for honesty of construction, fitness of materials and elegant simplicity. Versatile and durable, the chair no. 14 epitomised the anonymous product which fulfilled all the requirements of mass-consumption.

6   Rocking chair no. 511, white painted bentwood c.1905.

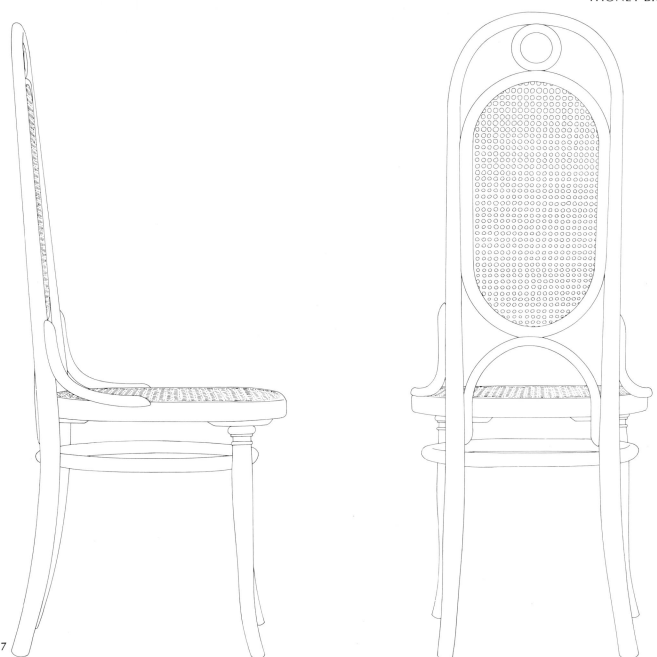

7   Chair no. 17, side and rear view. The chairs nos. 16 and 17 were the only Thonet designs with high backs, and were probably inspired by the English furniture exhibited at the 1862 London exhibition.

8   Armchair c.1840, produced during Thonet's period at Boppard.

9   Three upholstered bentwood chairs designed for the Liechtenstein Palace, Vienna c.1845. The chair on the left is gold-plated.

1   Armchair, beechwood stained olive brown and waxed with plywood seat and aluminium feet and rivets. Designed for the board room of the Austrian Postal Savings Bank in 1902, and subsequently manufactured by Kohn & Kohn and Thonet.
2   Armchair, beechwood lacquered in black and white with plywood seat. Manufactured by Thonet, and used in the Austrian Postal Savings Bank and the Second Villa Wagner, Vienna 1912-13.

Otto Koloman Wagner

1841-1918

Otto Koloman Wagner was the founder of the Vienna School and an influential precursor of twentieth-century architecture and town planning. Through his teaching at the Vienna Academy from 1894 he provided an open-minded and inspired training for pupils such as Joseph Maria Olbrich, Josef Hoffmann and Adolf Loos, and his inaugural lecture, published as *Moderne Architektur* in 1895, is generally hailed as the first important treatise on modern architecture.

Wagner studied civil engineering at the Vienna Polytechnic (1857-60) and architecture at the Bauakademie in Berlin and the Vienna Academy, graduating in 1863. Although his early work is marked by a historical outlook, his radical scheme for

the complete remodelling of the city of Vienna (1890) led him to be appointed as an advisor to the Viennese Transport Commission, for whom he designed buildings on the Danube Canal and the thirty-six stations of the Vienna Stadtbahn. His belief in the necessity for an architecture suited to the requirements of contemporary living, with form emerging naturally from a willing acceptance of new materials and technology, found concrete expression in buildings such as his Austrian Postal Savings Bank (1903-07) and Church am Steinhof (1905-07).

Like his architecture, Wagner's furniture designs show a desire to experiment with new techniques and an awareness of the practical requirements of the client.

Although his early buildings were usually furnished with reproduction pieces, by the turn of the century he was producing most of the furniture for his own schemes, in accordance with the Secession idea of *Gesamtkunstwerk* — the total work of art.

Wagner's most notable chair designs were for his Austrian Postal Savings Bank, for which he produced elegant yet practical chairs, stools and armchairs characterised by a use of aluminium bolts and caps for the feet — an echo, perhaps, of his concern to visibly expose the structure of the building throughout. The bentwood armchairs combine comfort with an economical use of material, and were among the first bentwood chairs to be used by a distinguished architect.

1

2

3

Koloman Moser

1869-1918

Austrian painter and designer, Koloman Moser studied in Vienna at the Academy of Creative Arts (1886-92) and the School of Arts and Crafts (1892-95). He was a founder member of the Vienna Secession in 1897, and his designs for Secession posters, exhibition catalogues and the monthly magazine *Ver Sacrum* helped to establish him as the leading Viennese graphic artist. In 1903, together with Josef Hoffmann, Moser founded the Wiener Werkstätte, for which he designed jewellery, glassware, silverware and furniture. He resigned in 1906, however, because of his objection to the increasing diversification of activities and dependence on the taste of the client. As a professor at the Vienna School of Arts and Crafts from 1900 to 1918 Moser was an

influential figure in the establishment of the Vienna School. He continued to work as a painter and illustrator throughout his life.

Moser was one of the first Viennese artists to reject the floral style of Art Nouveau, and he objected strongly to the increased use of ornamentation and floral decoration in the work of the Wiener Werkstätte after about 1905. He is also credited with the origination of the characteristic Secession black and white square motif, which he saw as 'a refreshing contrast to the false warmth of the upholsterers' art'.

Moser's chair designs are in a stringent, rectilinear style using highly polished woods. More characteristically Secessionist than much of the work of

Hoffmann, his designs exhibit a stark geometry, with strongly emphasised verticals and horizontals.

1   Upholstered armchair, 1904. Executed by the Wiener Werkstätte and exhibited at the group's 1905 exhibition.
2   White painted beechwood chair with aluminium capped feet and upholstered seat and back, 1903.
3   Dining chair, walnut inlaid with mahogany and sycamore and leather upholstery. Part of a dining-room suite executed in 1900 by August Ingethüm, Vienna.

1

2

Josef Hoffmann

1870-1956

Austrian architect, designer and craftsman, Josef Hoffmann was a co-founder in 1897 of the Vienna Secession and in 1903 of the Wiener Werkstätte — a group of workshops and studios which enjoyed widespread success for almost thirty years. A pupil of Otto Wagner, in whose studio he worked for a short time in 1895 on his return from a year in Italy as Prix de Rome scholar, Hoffmann's work combined the rationalism of Wagner with a geometrical, rectilinear style of decoration influenced by the work of Charles Rennie Mackintosh. During the years preceding the First World War he designed several villas in Vienna as well as his two masterpieces — the Purkersdorf Sanatorium (1903) and the Palais Stoclet, Brussels (1905-11). He was

appointed city architect of Vienna in 1920 and continued to work until after the Second World War, producing housing schemes in Vienna as well as pavilions for the 1914 Cologne Werkbund exhibition, the 1925 Paris exhibition and the Venice Biennale of 1934. Hoffmann taught at the Vienna School of Arts and Crafts from 1899 to 1937.

Hoffmann's first furniture designs were simple pieces with lattice decorations for Joseph Maria Olbrich's Secession Building of 1898. By 1900, however, in the furniture shown at the Paris exhibition, he had abandoned curvilinear decoration in favour of the angular forms, geometrical decoration and smooth surfaces which were to become the major characteristics

of the mature Secession style. The chair designs published in 1901 with his essay 'Einfache Möbel' (Simple Furniture) clearly derive from the work of Mackintosh, but add functional purpose to the latter's aesthetic achievements.

Hoffmann designed for the Weiner Werkstätte finely crafted, well-proportioned chairs whose cubistic forms and restricted colour schemes (primarily black and white) anticipated the stylistic preoccupations of the 1920s and 30s. The Werkstätte served a rich, sophisticated cosmopolitan clientele (such as the proprietor of the lavish Palais Stoclet), and worked on the principle that quality could only be obtained if each piece was personally designed and each step of its

4

3

5

creation supervised by the designer, with a total rejection of machine production. Hoffmann's designs for the Werkstätte thus unite extreme individuality and painstaking hand craftsmanship with the concern for truth to materials and functionalism which characterised all his work. As well as his Werkstätte chairs, Hoffmann also produced designs which were manufactured by Kohn & Kohn using the bentwood technique. Unlike his architecture, which was nicknamed *Quadratlstil* because of its relentless use of the square, Hoffmann's bentwood chairs exploit the circle as their major motif, and in particular a decorative use of spherical appendages to externally express the joints.

1   Side chair, 1901, beechwood stained black and polished with feet capped in aluminium. The seat and back are covered in leather, and edged by a border made up of the typical Secession black and white square motif.
2   Polished beechwood chair with plywood back and studded leather seat designed for the Purkersdorf Sanatorium in 1903 and

manufactured by Kohn & Kohn. The spherical appendages beneath the seat are a typical feature of Hoffmann's work.
3   Armchair, beechwood with mahogany stain, leather seat, 1905. This model was manufactured by both Thonet and Kohn & Kohn, who advertised it in their 1906 catalogue as part of a set of furniture called the 'Fledermausgarnitur'.
4   Adjustable armchair in polished beechwood with red mahogany stain and plywood seat, back and sides, 1905. The wooden spheres are here used structurally as supports for the brass bar attached to the back of the chair, which can be moved into a variety of reclining positions. An upholstered version was also produced.
5   Winged armchair on casters in polished beechwood with leather upholstery, 1904. Manufactured by Kohn & Kohn.

1

2

3

4

Joseph Urban

1872-1933

After training at the Vienna Academy from 1890 to 1893, Joseph Urban worked as an architect and designer in Vienna. He was an active member of the Künstlerhaus and the Siebenerclub and president of the Hagenbund from 1906 to 1908. In 1911 Urban emigrated to America, and from 1918 to 1933 he worked as chief designer at the Metropolitan Opera House, New York. During this period he directed over twenty films as well as several Broadway productions, while continuing his work in interior design through his own studio. He maintained his contact with Vienna, establishing a branch of the Wiener Werkstätte in New York in 1922.

Urban's chair designs of his Vienna period are characterised by a Secessionist use of strong geometrical forms, and sharp contrasts of black and white. His favoured wood was mahogany, which was usually stained black, with geometrical decoration inlaid in silver or ivory. He also produced some bentwood designs which were manufactured by Thonet.

1 Side chair in beechwood stained dark and polished, c.1902. The back and seat are covered in leather with brass studs, and the feet are capped in brass.
2 Room at the Vienna Hagenbund exhibition of 1903, arranged by Urban. The chairs with aluminium legs and mother-of-pearl inlay were executed by B. Ludwig to Urban's design.
3 Room at the Vienna Hagenbund exhibition of 1903. The chairs, in black mahogany inlaid with silver, were designed by Urban and executed by Karl Hans Jàray.
4 Room at the Vienna Hagenbund exhibition of 1906, which was arranged by Urban. The chairs were executed to Urban's designs by Sandor Jàray.

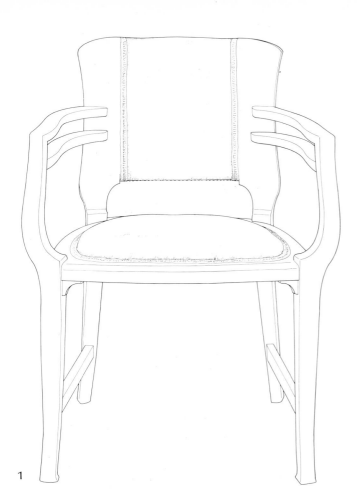

1 Upholstered mahogany armchair, c.1900. Executed by the Hofmöbelfabrik J. Glückert, Darmstadt and exhibited at the Paris 1900 exhibition.
2 Polished walnut armchair with carved back, brass inlay and upholstered seat, designed for the children's room of the Villa Friedmann, Hinterbrühl 1898.

Joseph Maria Olbrich

1867-1908

Joseph Maria Olbrich was a seminal figure in the foundation of two of the most important artistic developments of the final years of the nineteenth century — the Vienna Secession and the Darmstadt Artists' Colony. In a brief but prolific career of less than a decade, he produced over 150 buildings and projects in a style characterised by a combination of rational design and exuberant spontaneity to make him one of the most influential architects of the Jugendstil movement.

After studying at the Vienna Academy from 1890 to 1893 and visiting Italy and North Africa as winner of the Prix de Rome, Olbrich worked for four years in the studio of Otto Wagner, assisting in the design of the Stadtbahn stations. His major work in Vienna, the Secession Building (1898), was designed to house the group's exhibitions and its geometrical outlines mark the beginning of the Viennese interpretation of Art Nouveau. In 1899 Olbrich moved to Darmstadt at the invitation of Grand Duke Ernst Ludwig of Hesse, and over the next eight years he was almost solely responsible for the construction of the Darmstadt Artists' Colony, including several houses and studios as well as the spectacular Wedding Tower of 1905-08. His other major building in Germany, the Warenhaus Tietz in Düsseldorf, was still under construction at the time of his tragically early death from leukaemia.

Olbrich was attracted to Darmstadt in the hope of fulfilling the Secession ideal of *Gesamtkunstwerk* — a total work of art in which design would be a 'true reflection of modern culture in strong unshakeable forms developed from an up-to-date artistic sensitivity'. His chairs of both the Vienna and Darmstadt periods were designed as individual pieces for a specific setting, and reproduce in miniature the spirit and form of his architecture. Executed in wood with delicately carved decoration using abstract-organic motifs, Olbrich's designs are characterised by simple, strong lines and gently curving forms.

1

Richard Riemerschmid

1868-1957

Richard Riemerschmid began his career as a painter, studying art at the Munich Academy from 1888 to 1890. Like many of his contemporaries, however, he soon became involved in the applied arts, and in 1897 was a co-founder of the Vereinigte Werkstätten für Kunst und Handwerk — the Munich Secession group. He also played an important role in the formation of the Deutscher Werkbund in 1907. As well as the furniture, fabrics, glassware, silverware and ceramics he designed for the Vereinigte Werkstätten, Riemerschmid also produced some architectural schemes including a house for his family at Pasing near Munich (1896), the 'Room of an Art Lover' for the Paris 1900 exhibition, interiors for the Munich Schauspielhaus

(1901) and plans for the garden city which grew up around the Deutscher Werkbund in Dresden-Hellerau (1909). He held the post of director of the Munich Kunstgewerbeschule from 1913 to 1924 and in 1926 established the Werkschule in Cologne.

Riemerschmid's early work, such as the side chair and armchair of 1899, is characterised by a simple, unornamented elegance and represents a highly functional, organic solution to the problem of chair design which anticipates Danish work of the post-War period. Certain of his designs, such as the armchair of 1900, also show the influence of traditional German arts and crafts, and this particular piece, with its flat surfaces and geometrical symmetry is a perfect synthesis of local

tradition and urban elegance.

Riemerschmid's major contribution, however, was in his pioneering of machine-made furniture for the Vereinigte Werkstätten, who as a group were concerned with the production of inexpensive, high quality furniture for as wide a public as possible. Riemerschmid's first machine-made chairs were produced in the Dresden workshops of his brother-in-law Karl Schmidt in 1905, according to prototypes designed specifically for machine production in 1902. Accepting that at the time machines were not accurate enough to cut wood to fit exactly into a tongue-and-groove joint, Riemerschmid designed his chairs so that all the joints overlapped and could be screwed into place, which

2

3

had the additional advantage of enabling the furniture to be transported to its destination in pieces and assembled on arrival. The designs were made in three price-ranges — the cheapest being in pine — and initially changed every year because of Schmidt's fear that the public would not accept mass-production on such a large scale.

In 1909, Riemerschmid took machine production even further in the creation of his 'Typenmöbel', in collaboration with K. Bertsch. The 'Typenmöbel' involved carefully worked out and tested types of construction whereby the individual parts were virtually interchangeable — one form of arm, for example, could be replaced on the same basic chair by a variety of others.

Bertsch and Riemerschmid evolved over 800 possible combinations, and although the chairs were made cheaply and in large quantities, Riemerschmid claimed that the process ensured that each chair had an 'individuality and character of its own, without betraying the use of machinery in its production'.

1   Oak side chair with leather seat exhibited in a music room at the Dresden exhibition of 1899 and at the Paris exhibition of 1900.
2, 3 Mahogany armchair and dining chair designed for the house of the banker Karl von Thieme, Munich 1903 and executed by Kohlbecker & Sohn, Munich.
4   Music room presented at the 1899 Dresden exhibition.

4

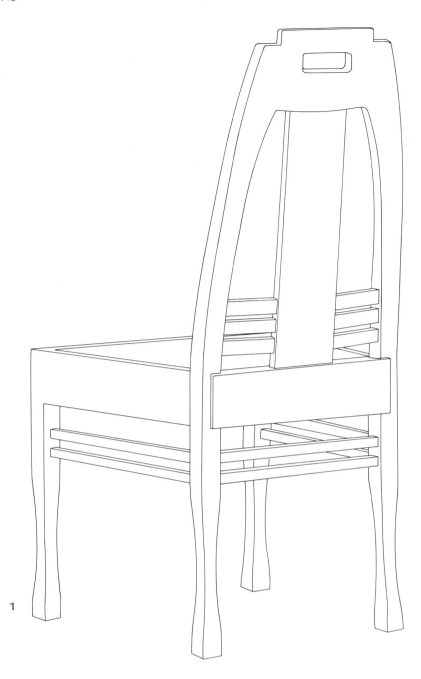

1

2

3

4

Peter Behrens

1868-1940

Peter Behrens began his career as a painter, studying at art schools in Karlsruhe and Düsseldorf from 1886 to 1889 and joining the Munich Secession in 1893. He was a co-founder of the Munich Vereinigte Werkstätten für Kunst und Handwerk in 1897, and two years later joined the Darmstadt Artists' Colony where he made his first experiments in the field of architecture and interior design with the construction of his own house in 1901.

Behrens was one of the first architects of the twentieth century to develop a form of architectural thought which would meet the demands of an industrialised nation, and the factories, houses and offices he built in Germany, together with his work in the field of industrial design for the Berlin electrical company AEG established him as an important figure in the Modern Movement. He held several teaching posts including those of director of the Düsseldorf School of Art (1903-07), director of the School of Architecture at the Vienna Academy (from 1922) and head of the department of architecture at the Prussian Academy in Berlin (from 1936), and counted Mies van der Rohe, Walter Gropius and Le Corbusier among his pupils.

Behrens was the only member of the Darmstadt Artists' Colony other than Joseph Maria Olbrich to practise architecture, and he designed all the furniture and fittings for his own house down to the smallest detail. His chairs of the Darmstadt period are all in wood, and rely for their effect on strong simple lines with upholstery either in plain fabric or using dramatic geometric patterns. Occasionally, as in the dining-room chairs for his own house, his work shows affinities with the designs of Henry van de Velde.

1   Polished beechwood dining chair, 1902.
2   Dining room of the Haus Behrens, Darmstadt 1901. The chairs and sofa in white lacquered poplar wood were executed by J. D. Heymann of Hamburg.
3   Music room of the Haus Behrens, with stools and chairs in black stained birch inlaid with other stained woods.
4   Library of the Haus Behrens. The desk chair in natural elm was made by C. J. Peter of Mannheim.

The Munich Group

In the early 1890s Munich was the major creative centre, in Germany, and the meeting place for an influential group of artists and craftsmen which included Peter Behrens, Otto Eckmann, August Endell, Hermann Obrist, Bernhard Pankok, Bruno Paul and Richard Riemerschmid. Although by the turn of the century the group had largely disbanded, Munich nevertheless remained the original home of the German Jugendstil movement, and the centre of the floral style.

Hermann Obrist 1863-1927

Hermann Obrist discovered his characteristic style, epitomised by the 'Whiplash' wall hanging of 1895, through the medium of embroidery, and it was an exhibition of his work in 1894 which marked the beginning of the Jugendstil movement. He was a co-founder in 1897 of the Vereinigte Werkstätten für Kunst und Handwerk, a group of Munich craftsmen whose aim was to produce furniture of high formal quality for a vast public. Olbrist's chairs are characterised by the use of the simple yet dynamic lines of his embroidery, and have the curious knobbly joints seen in the work of Endell.

August Endell 1871-1925

Like most of his fellow Munich artists, August Endell was extremely versatile, designing furniture, carpets and jewellery as well as architectural commissions such as the Atelier Elvira (1897-98) which was noteworthy for the dramatic decorative relief of its façade. His chair designs use traditional materials, such as elm, upholstered in brightly-coloured fabrics of geometrical design. Their forms are the characteristic sweeping curves of Jugendstil, interspersed with curious pointed angles and knobbly joints.

Otto Eckmann 1865-1902

Otto Eckmann was widely recognised as the undisputed master of floral Jugendstil through his graphic work for the German magazines *Pan* and *Die Jugend,* and later became the first German artist to achieve the abstract dynamism of Belgian Art Nouveau. From about 1897, as professor at the Kunstgewerbeschule in Berlin, he devoted himself increasingly to the applied arts, designing textiles, furniture, rugs and complete interiors, including commissions for Grand Duke Ernst Ludwig of Hesse. His chairs are essentially simple designs in wood which reflect the dynamic lines of his graphic work.

1   ECKMANN Stained gaboon and maple armchair with upholstered seat, c.1900.
2   OBRIST Oak dining chair with upholstered seat and back from the Heiseler family house, Brannenburg c.1898.
3   ENDELL Elm writing chair with upholstery designed by Richard Riemerschmid from the Heiseler family house, Brannenburg c.1900.

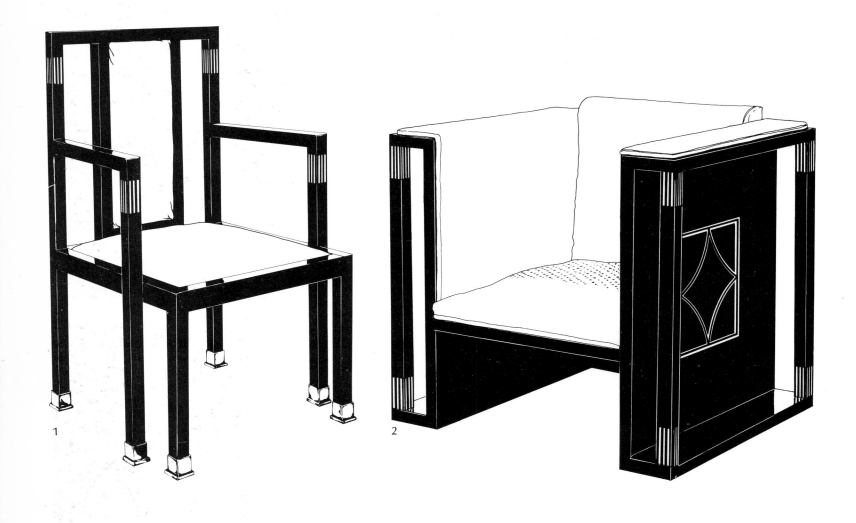

1

2

Hans Christiansen

1866-1945

Hans Christiansen studied painting in Hamburg and at the Kunstgewerbeschule in Munich, and in 1890 founded a company dealing in paintings and interior decoration in Hamburg. As a representative of the Deutsche Reich aus Hamburg he visited the 1893 Columbian World's Exhibition in Chicago where the work of Louis Comfort Tiffany had a profound effect on his own ideas. This was followed by a further period of study — in Antwerp in 1895, and at the Académie Julian in Paris from 1896 to 1899 — as well as two exhibitions in Darmstadt. From 1899 to 1902 Christiansen was a member of the Darmstadt Artists' Colony, and from 1902 to 1911 he divided his time between Darmstadt and Paris. He retired to Wiesbaden in 1911, where he spent the rest

of his life as a painter and writer of philosophy.

Christiansen, like his fellow members of the Artists' Colony, believed in the synthesis of the arts to create an harmonious totality, and himself practised in several media including glass, ceramics, silverware, carpets, jewellery, furniture and fashion design. His chairs vary enormously in accordance with the context for which they were designed, as can be seen by a comparison of two sets of chairs for his own Wiesbaden house — the highly ornate, gilt salon chairs and the more characteristic living room chairs which are reminiscent of the work of the Vienna Secessionists in their stark geometry, dramatic contrast of colours and metal capped feet.

1 Upholstered side chair designed for the living room of Christiansen's Wiesbaden house, c.1911, in beechwood stained black and polished, with inlays of Brazilian rosewood. The original upholstery was green, black and grey stripes.
2 Companion armchair.

2

3

Hector Guimard

1867-1942

Hector Guimard was the leading French architect of the Art Nouveau style, and was responsible for introducing the Belgian Art Nouveau of Victor Horta to Paris. His work is highly individual, with a rational approach to structure and willing use of new materials — in particular cast iron — which raise it above the fashionable façade decoration of many of his Parisian contemporaries.

Guimard studied at both the Ecole des Arts Décoratifs and the Ecole des Beaux-Arts. In 1894 he travelled to England where he was introduced to the work of the domestic revival, and during a visit to Brussels the following year the impression made on him by Victor Horta's Maison Tassel inspired him to redesign the details

of his Castel Béranger, which became the first and most complete manifesto of his personal style. Guimard's work reached its peak at the turn of the century with such buildings as the Humbert de Romans concert hall, Paris (1897-1901), the Maison Coilliot, Lille (1898-1900), the Castel Henriette, Sèvres (1899) and his cast iron and glass entrances for the Paris metro. He continued to design into the 1930s, but died in relative obscurity in New York.

Throughout his career Guimard remained faithful to the idea of architecture as an all-embracing art, and he devoted as much time to interior as to exterior, designing floor and wall coverings, light fixtures, doors, windows, fireplaces and furniture for his buildings. His chairs,

which were always designed for a specific context with the aim of creating an harmonious totality, are essentially traditional in form, and gain their effect from a decorative rather than structural use of carved wood to give the impression of sinuous, organic curves.

1   Pearwood chair with elaborate carved detail and embossed leather upholstery.
2   Dining chair, designed for Guimard's own house in the avenue Mozart, Paris 1909-12.
3   Side chair in carved wood with embossed leather upholstery.

4　　　　　5　　　　　6　　　　　7

8

9　　　　10

4　　Side chair in cherry wood with plush upholstery, designed for a room in Guimard's own house, probably the bedroom, c.1912.
5　　Pearwood chair, designed for the Hôtel Nozal, Paris 1902-05.
6　　Side chair, designed for the Maison Coilliot, Lille 1898-1900.
7　　Armchair, designed for the Maison Coilliot.
8　　Mahogany sofa with embossed leather upholstery, designed for the Castel Béranger, Paris 1894-98 and later used in the Maison Coilliot.
9　　Banquette from the Castel Béranger, 1897-98.
10　　Bedroom of Guimard's own house.

Opposite
Armchair in carved wood with embossed leather upholstery.

1

2

3

4

1

2

3

4

The Nancy School

5

6

7

The Nancy School was an alliance of Lorraine artists and architects who officially joined forces in 1901 as the 'Ecole de Nancy, Alliance Provinciale des Industries d'Art' with Emile Gallé as their first president. The group, which included Victor Prouvé, Louis Majorelle, Jacques Gruber, Emile André and Eugène Vallin, exhibited together until 1909, and was one of the most innovative forces in the French Art Nouveau movement.

Emile Gallé 1846-1904

Although Emile Gallé worked primarily in the fields of glassware and ceramics, his furniture, produced from about 1884, was to have a widespread influence on his contemporaries. Gallé claimed that the idea of creating furniture came to him in 1884 when he visited a stockist of exotic woods in search of an exquisite base for a piece of his glassware. Within a year he had added a fully staffed and equipped cabinet-making factory to his father's ceramics and glassware company, producing both specially commissioned furniture — whose marquetry could involve over fifty pieces of wood and take years to make — and smaller pieces which could be made inexpensively with the help of machines.

Gallé believed that 'modernity, far from involving stylistic novelty and self-assertiveness, is simply tailoring furniture to suit present needs', and he saw himself as a rational force among his contemporaries. His chairs are exclusively in wood, waxed rather than varnished or polished to achieve a natural effect, and are of conventional construction, relying on historical styles. Their individuality lies in their ornamentation, with flat surfaces treated as blank canvases on which to elaborate floral themes either in high-relief moulding or through a subtle juxtaposition of rich woods.

Louis Majorelle 1859-1926

After training as a painter Louis Majorelle took over his father's cabinet-making and ceramics business in 1879, and soon dedicated most of his time to furniture, designing furniture and fittings for the Parisian restaurants Chez Maxim, Lucas Carton and the Café de Paris. Although his early work was in the Louis XV manner favoured by his father, he was soon encouraged by the success of Emile Gallé to evolve a more personal style. At their best his chair designs, executed in hard woods such as mahogany or walnut, are a perfect expression of the abstract-organic style of Art Nouveau, with rounded ample forms decorated with high-relief mouldings, marquetry and gilt bronze mounts.

Eugène Vallin 1856-1922

The work of the architect, sculptor and cabinet-maker Eugène Vallin bears the mark of his solid training as an ecclesiastical cabinet-maker with his uncle, and his designs are closer to the heavy, sculptural forms of Hector Guimard than any other designer of the Nancy School. Executed in

8

9

wood, his furniture is massively carved with powerful organic lines, giving an impression of majesty and monumental scale.

1 GALLE Dining chair, c.1901-02, walnut with pink plush upholstery, part of a set of twelve from the house of Edouard Hannon in Brussels.
2 MAJORELLE Walnut armchair, designed before 1900 as part of a set which included a sofa with the same carved decoration and delicate upholstery.

3 MAJORELLE Oak dining chair with green plush upholstery and carved decoration.
4 MAJORELLE Mahogany desk chair with embossed leather upholstery c.1900.
5 MAJORELLE Side chair in carved wood with upholstered seat and back.
6 MAJORELLE Carved oak armchair, c.1900.
7 VALLIN Dining chair with leather upholstery. A similar model was used in the dining-room of the Nancy house of M. Masson, c.1903-05.
8 MAJORELLE Green stained walnut armchair with back and seat covered in embroidered and painted mauve satin, c.1900.
9 GALLE Beechwood side chair upholstered in pale yellow and pink cut velvet from the Edouard Hannon house, Brussels, c.1902. The 'ombelle' motif, which also appears in a matching sofa and footstool, was inspired by a Japanese sword-guard.

François Rupert Carabin

1862-1932

Carabin left his native Alsace in 1872 to move with his family to Paris. The following year he began to make a living carving cameos, and later he learned woodcarving from a sculptor in the Faubourg Saint-Antoine. His work was exhibited at the Salon des Indépendants from its opening in 1884 and from 1890 he produced jewellery, medals and ceramics with Jean Carriès and a number of sculptures including the famous Loïe Fuller figurines (1896-97). In 1914 he gave up his work in art, and in 1920 became director of the Ecole des Arts Décoratifs in Strasbourg.

To Carabin furniture was sculpture on which the artist could impose his own laws, and in this he broke with a tradition unquestioned since the Renaissance which saw furniture as taking its structure and ornament from architecture. Although at one with his contemporaries in his desire to break down the traditional barriers between the arts, he was contemptuous of the 'macaroni style' of Horta and Guimard, which he felt had 'arrested the French movement launched by some few artists earlier'.

Carabin's first commission was a walnut bookcase designed for Henry Montandon in 1889, with realistic carved female nudes representing a Reader, Truth, Reflection and Ignorance. The bookcase gave Carabin the opportunity to realise his highly individual conception of furniture

1

design, and his subsequent chair designs are characterised by a similar sculptural, often allegorical, use of the female nude. Executed almost exclusively in wood — pear, oak and especially walnut — their rich patina was achieved by patient hand rubbing with linseed oil for hours at a time.

1   Carved mahogany chair (as illustrated on page 73) with a characteristic use of the female nude, c.1896, together with a matching table in which the table top, in the form of a massive book, is supported by two nude female figures.
2   Walnut chair, 1895, exhibited at the Société Nationale des Beaux-Arts in 1896. This chair illustrates Carabin's conception of furniture as sculpture, with the carved figures forming an integral part of the structure of the chair.

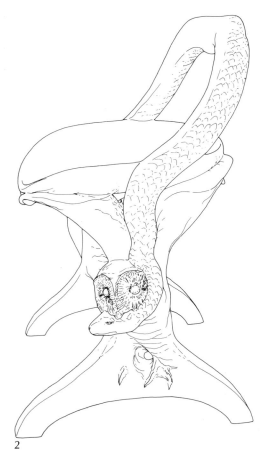

2

Eugène Gaillard

1862-1933

Eugène Gaillard began his career as a lawyer, and then spent ten years as a sculptor before devoting his time exclusively to interior design. He was one of the principal collaborators of Samuel Bing's L'Art Nouveau, and contributed the bedroom and dining-room to Bing's Pavillon de l'Art Nouveau at the Paris 1900 exhibition, an ensemble of six fully decorated rooms designed by Gaillard, Georges de Feure and Edward Colonna.

Gaillard defined his aims in his essay *A propos du Mobilier,* published in 1906, as 'to put an undeniable artistic character into the most humble object, the ordinary piece of furniture', and 'to furnish beautiful prototypes of all kinds for the so-called art industries'. A rationalist and purist,

primarily interested in structure, he used the plastic curves of Art Nouveau to create refined, and at the same time, solid and comfortable furniture with an emphasis on flowing lines and correct proportions. His chair designs are mostly in hard woods — mahogany, Brazilian rosewood and walnut — with tooled leather panels or silk upholstery decorated with graphic patterns which complement the flowing rhythm of the whole. Unlike many of his contemporaries, he avoided a figurative representation of nature, believing that decoration should be 'unreal. . . so that it might be completely natural without evoking any precise form from the animal or vegetable kingdoms'.

On colour page 72
1   Mahogany side chair with leather upholstery, before 1900. According to Gaillard, this was the first chair he designed for Samuel Bing's L'Art Nouveau.
2   Mahogany chair with embossed leather upholstery, c.1899-1900.
3   Dining chair in polished walnut designed for Samuel Bing's Pavillon de l'Art Nouveau at the Paris 1900 exhibition.
4   Dining-room of Samuel Bing's Pavillon de l'Art Nouveau at the Paris 1900 exhibition. The chairs are in polished walnut with bronze fittings and embossed leather upholstery.

1

Georges de Feure

1868-1928

Georges de Feure was one of the most diversely talented artists of the turn of the century, and in the course of his career he worked as a painter, lithographer, engraver, ceramist, interior designer, and later as professor at the Ecole des Beaux-Arts in Paris. De Feure left his native Holland in 1890 to study painting in Paris in the studio of Jules Chéret, and subsequently exhibited at the Société Nationale des Beaux-Arts (1894), the salons of the Rose + Croix (1893 and 1894), and the 1896 Munich Secession. During this period he also produced illustrations for the periodicals *Le Courrier Français* and *Le Boulevard,* sets for productions at Le Chat Noir, and several posters, the most successful of which presented a pale, mysterious woman, the fin-de-siècle femme fatale, rendered with sophistication and sinister symbolist overtones using muted colours of brown, green and rose. De Feure's work in the field of applied arts included designs for stained-glass, furniture and porcelain, often for Samuel Bing. The white porcelain with green and mauve decorations he exhibited at the Société Nationale des Beaux-Arts in 1901 and the Turin exhibition of 1902 won him widespread critical acclaim.

In 1898 de Feure designed furniture for the Maison Fleury, and he later collaborated with Edward Colonna and Eugène Gaillard in the design of Bing's Pavillon de l'Art Nouveau at the Paris 1900 exhibition. His chairs are an elegant combination of the traditional and the modern, executed in wood and often gilded, or lacquered and upholstered in his favoured colours of green and rose. Their organic lines are complimented by a restrained use of motifs or forms inspired by nature, as in the sofa with a back in the form of a butterfly's wings and his widespread use of the poppy flower as carved or inlaid ornament.

1   Gilt ash sofa with silk upholstery designed for the boudoir of Samuel Bing's Pavillon de l'Art Nouveau at the Paris 1900 exhibition. The back of the sofa is in the form of a butterfly's wings.

1

Victor Horta

1861-1946

Victor Horta was the major Belgian exponent of Art Nouveau, and his work of the 1890s initiated a new style of architecture which totally rejected nineteenth-century canons of design. Through a series of private houses, department stores and public buildings in and around Brussels he developed his original vocabulary of ornament and total, organic conception of architecture, in which structure, decoration and furniture combined to produce an effect of overwhelming unity. His work also opened new paths to twentieth-century architecture through his exploration of the open plan and his innovative use of exposed structures of iron and glass.

Horta trained at the Académie des Beaux-Arts in Brussels before joining the office of the neo-classical architect Alphonse Balat. His first major work — the Maison Tassel of 1893 — was the first recognisably Art Nouveau house in Europe, and was followed by several commissions including the Hôtel Solvay (1894) and Hôtel van Eetvelde (1897-1900). Horta belonged to the circle of artists, architects and intellectuals who formed the nucleus of the Belgian Socialist Party, and in 1895 he was given the task of designing their new headquarters, the Maison du Peuple, whose iron and glass façade was the first of its kind to be built in Belgium. Although he continued to build until about 1910, he acknowledged in his Mémoires that his work reached its peak in the design for his own house and studio (1898). The latter part of his life was

taken up by two major commissions — the Palais des Beaux-Arts (1919-28) and the Gare Centrale (1937-52) — as well as several academic posts including that of director of the Académie des Beaux-Arts (1912-31).

Horta's work epitomised the best of Art Nouveau architecture, with structure, glasswork, decoration and furniture combining to form an harmonious totality employing a whiplash graphicism and energetic curves. Although the furniture for the Maison Tassel was bought from English Arts and Crafts firms, Horta took great pains to design every element of his subsequent commissions, regarding the interior decoration of his houses as 'a joyous rest after the worry of construction'. His

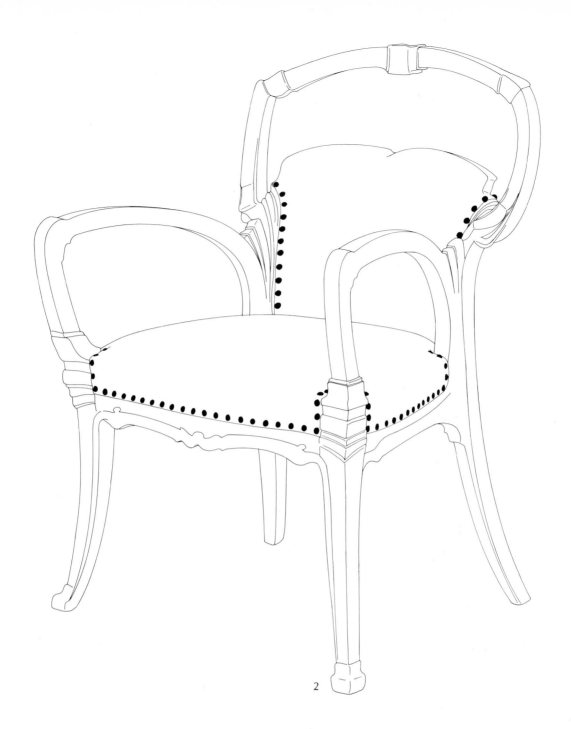

2

furniture owes much to traditional French cabinet-making techniques, with an architect's concern for sound construction. Executed in hard woods with rich upholstery and an emphasis on comfort, its innovation lies in its abstract curving lines of organic force, based, Horta claimed, not on the flower or leaf, but on the stalk.

1   Mahogany side chair with silk velvet upholstery designed for the living room of the Hôtel Solvay, Brussels, c.1894.
2   Maple upholstered armchair, designed for the Turin exhibition of 1902.
3   Interior of the Hôtel Solvay, avenue Louise, Brussels 1894.

3

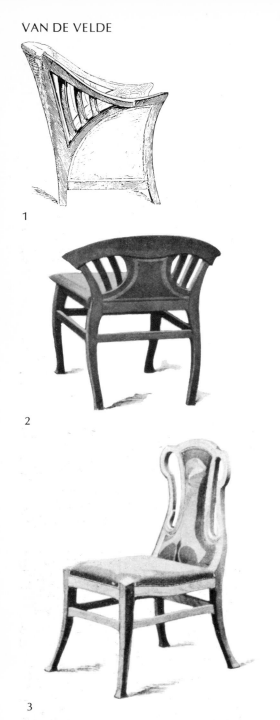

1

2

3

4

Henry-Clément van de Velde

1863-1957

Henry van de Velde was one of the most influential figures in the fields of architecture and the applied arts in the first quarter of the twentieth century, particularly in Germany. Like many of his contemporaries he began his career as a painter, studying in Antwerp and Paris and subsequently collaborating in the avantgarde artistic groups Als ik Kan (1886), L'Art Indépendant (1887) and Les Vingt (1889). In 1893 he renounced painting for the applied arts, and two years later was able to build his own house, Bloemenwerf, near Brussels, in which he designed every element himself to produce an organic whole. Bloemenwerf was visited by several influential people, including Samuel Bing, who in 1895 commissioned van de Velde to design four

rooms for his shop and gallery L'Art Nouveau, and Julius Meier-Graefe, who ordered furniture for La Maison Moderne and introduced van de Velde to the *Pan* group in Berlin, where he received several commissions for shops, houses and a museum.

Van de Velde had worked as artistic counsellor to the Grand Duke of Saxe-Weimar from 1901, and from 1906 until 1914 he was director of the Weimar Kunstgewerbeschule — later part of the Bauhaus — whose buildings he designed himself. He continued his work in architecture and the applied arts until the outbreak of the Second World War, and held teaching posts as first director of the Institut Supérieur des Arts Décoratifs de La

Cambre, Brussels (1926-35) and as professor at the University of Ghent (1926-36). In 1947 he settled in Oberägeri, Switzerland, and devoted his time to writing his memoirs.

Van de Velde's first work in three dimensions was in the field of furniture design and by 1898 his interest had stimulated him to open his own cabinet-making workshop near Brussels — the Société van de Velde. Despite his apparent modernism, however, van de Velde ran his workshop in accordance with the principles of William Morris and John Ruskin, and the expensive methods of manufacture, with an almost exclusive use of hand craftsmanship, meant that the Société was often near financial ruin and

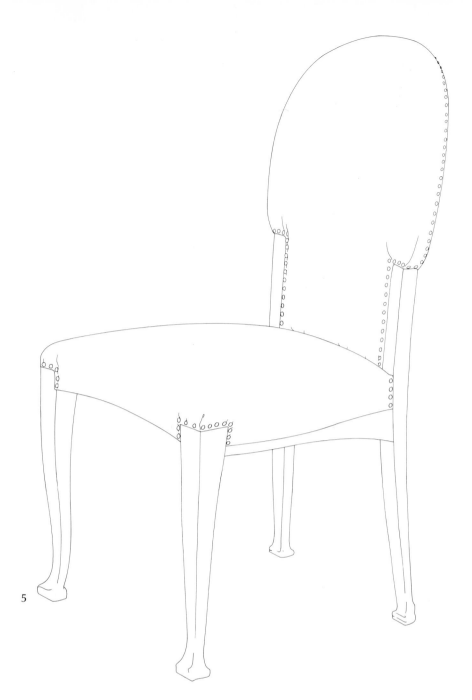

5

6

7

8

9

their output only accessible to a wealthy élite.

On questions of style, however, van de Velde was more rigorous than any other Art Nouveau artist in his rejection of elements from the past, and he turned away from floral forms early in his career to a more abstract-organic style. His chair designs are a perfect expression of his maxim 'the line is a force', and gain their effect from the juxtaposition of dynamic lines and filled planes or voids. They owe much to the work of Gustave Serrurier-Bovy, and each structural element is functionally emphasised in accordance with van de Velde's belief that whatever the medium, the process of manufacture should be displayed 'proudly and frankly'.

1 Upholstered armchair from the Havana Company cigar shop, Berlin 1899-1900.
2 Upholstered mahogany chair presented as part of a bedroom suite at the La Haye salon.
3 Upholstered ash chair, presented as part of a dining-room suite at the Arts and Crafts salon, La Haye.
4 Oak side chair with rush seat, 1895-96, designed for the dining-room of van de Velde's own house, Bloemenwerf, near Brussels.
5 Dining chair in upholstered Macassar ebony, designed c.1900 and used in van de Velde's Haus Hohenhof, Hagen 1906.
6 Havana Company cigar shop.
7 Haby barber's shop, Berlin 1900-01.
8 Study of the Berlin apartment of M. le Directeur St.
9 Desk and chair designed for Julius Meier-Graefe, c.1897 and exhibited as part of a study at the Munich Secession exhibition of 1899.

1

4

3

2

Gustave Serrurier-Bovy

1848-1910

A Belgian designer and architect, Gustave Serrurier studied architecture at the academy in Liège before resuming his family's traditional profession of cabinet-making. In 1884 he travelled to England where he discovered the work of the Arts and Crafts movement and later in the same year he opened a furniture shop in Liège with his wife Marie Bovy, selling products from Japan and from Liberty's in London. From about 1890, Serrurier-Bovy began to design simple furniture to be made by artisans on the premises and in 1900 he opened a large, industrialised furniture factory, with outlets in Nice, La Haye, and Paris. His designs were influential during his lifetime, and he participated in several exhibitions including the first Salon de la

Libre Esthétique (1894), L'Oeuvre Artistique, Liège (1895), and the Salon du Champs de Mars, Paris (1896-1903).

Serrurier-Bovy's chair designs combine rigorous structural requirements with the simple, organic lines and slenderness of parts found in the work of Henry van de Velde. As with the work of Baillie Scott or Morris & Co., they can be divided into two categories — designs for rich clientele and sturdy well-made workers' furniture. It is his workers' furniture which brought him most recognition, however, and his complete interiors such as the study presented at the Salon de la Libre Esthétique in 1894 or his 'chambre d'artisan' of the following year received much attention in foreign pub-

lications. Serrurier-Bovy's contribution to the Liège exhibition of 1905 — a range of simple workers' furniture in birchwood which could be easily assembled by the client — is an early example of design for mass-production.

1   Oak dining chair with leather upholstery exhibited at the Salon du Champ de Mars, Paris in 1899.
2   'Chambre d'artisan', exhibited at the Salon de la Libre Esthétique in 1895.
3   Dining-room, exhibited at the Salon du Champ de Mars in 1899.
4   Study, exhibited at the Salon de la Libre Esthétique in 1894.

Ernesto Basile and Vittorio Ducrot

Vittorio Ducrot began his career in the early 1890s as an assistant to Carlo Golia, the representative in Palermo of the Torinese firm Solei Herbert & Co. and an importer of French and English furniture. By the time he met the architect Ernesto Basile in 1898, Ducrot was in charge of an interior design workshop of some 200 employees, and he subsequently recruited Basile as chief designer for his furniture, and the painter Ettore de Maria Bergler as a decorative artist.

Basile and Ducrot collaborated on several important works in the Italian Liberty style including the Villino Florio, Palermo (1899-1903) and the Grand Hotel Villa Igea of the same date — a combination of conventional revivalist exteriors and rich, Floreale interiors executed by Ducrot. By the time of the Turin 1902 exhibition or the 'sala meridionale' designed for the Venice exhibition of 1903, however, Basile-Ducrot were designing for mass-production, and their work shows the elegant unornamented simplicity found in the machine-made furniture of Richard Riemerschmid and the Deutscher Werkbund.

1   Armchair with leather seat based on a chair exhibited as part of a studio at the 1902 Turin exhibition, which was adapted and simplified for mass-production.
2   Armchair with leather seat, c.1900, designed for the Grand Hotel Villa Igea, Palermo 1899-1903.
3   Dining-room of the Grand Hotel Villa Igea.

3

2

3

1

Eugenio Quarti

1867-1931

4

5

The Italian interior designer and cabinet-maker Eugenio Quarti first trained as a cabinet-maker in Paris, and in 1890 moved to Milan to work with Carlo Bugatti. He exhibited work at the Turin exhibitions of 1898 and 1902, the Paris 1900 exhibition and the Milan exhibition of 1906. In about 1902 Quarti established his own business in Milan, working in all areas of interior design from tapestries to metalwork. His more important commissions include collaboration with the Liberty architect Giuseppe Sommaruga on the Palazzo Castiglioni, Milan (1901-03) and the interiors of both the Villa Carosio, Baveno (1908-09) and the Hôtel Bristol Palace, Genoa.

Quarti was the most important Italian 'Modernismo' cabinet-maker, and his work for the Turin 1898 exhibition, which combined the craftsman simplicity of Serrurier-Bovy with a traditional Italian feeling for luxury, was used as late as 1904 by the Italian magazine *Arte Italiana Decorativa e Industriale* to exemplify the 'nouvo stile'. Quarti's work reached its peak at the Turin 1902 exhibition, for which he produced chairs which combined the sinuous lines of Art Nouveau with rich inlays inspired perhaps by his period of training with Carlo Bugatti. In his subsequent furnishings for the bourgeois Milanese houses, Quarti lost some of his Modernismo inventiveness, using more austere, simple lines and rich materials akin to the French Art Deco of the 1920s.

1 Side chair in white maple with inlays of olivewood designed for the Hôtel Bristol Palace, Genoa c.1904. A companion armchair, heavier in form was also designed, and the pair were produced in small series for the furnishings of inns and hotels.
2 Drawing room presented at the Paris 1900 exhibition.
3 Bedroom presented at the Turin exhibition of 1898.
4 Bedroom, c.1905, with a version of the white maple side chair in illustration 1.
5 Dining-room presented at the Turin exhibition of 1898.

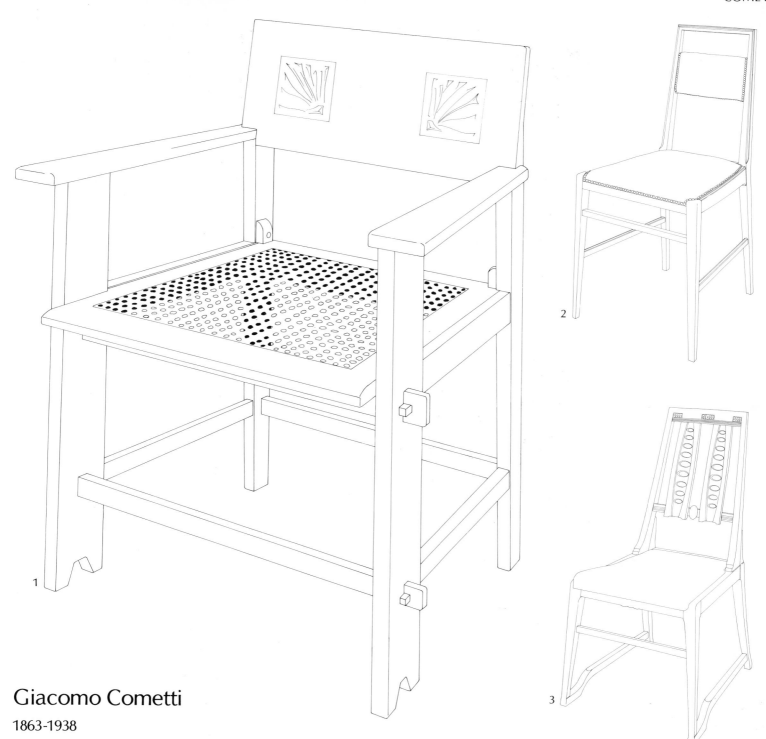

Giacomo Cometti

1863-1938

Giacomo Cometti was a member of the circle of artists and architects working in Turin at the turn of the century, and a disciple of the designer Leonardo Bistolfi, with whom he collaborated in 1900 on designs for a young ladies' room. He first came to public notice at the Paris 1900 exhibition and contributed decorative fountains to the Turin exhibition of 1902. Cometti's work as an interior designer included collaboration in the decoration of the offices of Gio. Porcheddu, the design of the dining-room for the Casa Coppa, Novara, and his most important work, the interiors and furnishings of Annibale Rigotti's Villa Falcioni at Domodossola (1903-04). He also designed fabrics and silverware, and opened a retailing company in Turin to distribute his work. Later in his life he moved towards an Art Deco style, as can be seen in the furniture exhibited at the 1st Triennale at Monza.

Cometti's chair designs are in wood, upholstered in rich fabrics with Floreale designs. They are characterised by simple, almost classical lines reminiscent of the early work of Peter Behrens and Henry van de Velde.

1   Armchair with carved wooden back and cane seat, c.1920-30.
2   Side chair with upholstered seat and back, c.1900-10.
3   Side chair with upholstered seat and carved back, c.1900-10.
4   Dining-room suite, c.1900-10.

1

Alphonse Marie Mucha

1860-1939

Alphonse Mucha was the most fashionable decorative artist in Paris at the turn of the century, and his sinuous, languid designs with their muted colours and perennial themes of women and flowers epitomise the taste of the belle époque.

Mucha left his native Czechoslovakia to become an apprentice scene painter in Vienna, and subsequently studied painting at the Munich Academy and the Académies Julian and Colarossi in Paris. From 1889 he earned his living as an illustrator and in 1894 enjoyed overnight success with a poster created for the actress Sarah Bernhardt, who offered him a six-year contract which in turn led to numerous commercial commissions for posters, calendars, lithographs and various kinds of advertising. As well as his graphic art, Mucha also designed jewellery, textiles and bronzes in collaboration with the sculptor Auguste Seysses. In 1901 he created an entire decorative scheme for the jeweller Georges Fouquet's shop in Paris, including delicate, sinuous furniture in walnut and fruitwood with leather upholstery and bronze mounts.

1 Chair design from *Documents Décoratifs,* a folio of Mucha's work in the applied arts published in 1902.
2 Walnut stool with gilt leather upholstery and delicate lattice carving designed for the jewellery shop of Georges Fouquet, Paris 1901.

2

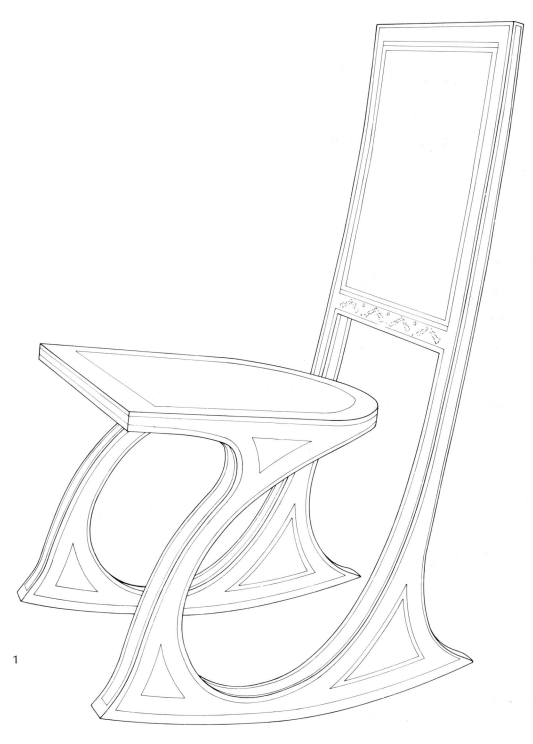

1

Carlo Bugatti

1856-1940

Carlo Bugatti studied at the Brera Academy in Milan and at the Ecole des Beaux-Arts in Paris, where he specialised in architecture before opening his own cabinet-making workshop and retailers in Milan in 1888. His furniture and interior designs were widely admired, and were awarded the silver medal at the Paris 1900 exhibition and the diploma of honour at the Turin exhibition of 1902. Bugatti moved to Paris in 1904, where he continued to accept furniture commissions, counting the stores Maison Dufayel and Au Bon Marché among his patrons. He also produced designs for a series of inventive stringed instruments and jewellery, as well as silverware which was exhibited at the Galérie Hébrard in 1907. Bugatti retired to Pierrefonds in 1910, and

subsequently played a large part in the local community, acting as Mayor during the First World War. His sons Rembrandt and Ettore are well known for their work in the fields of sculpture and car design respectively.

Carlo Bugatti was the only Italian designer to gain international recognition in a period dominated by the creative centres of Paris, Vienna, Brussels, Darmstadt and Glasgow. An extreme in-dividualist, he regarded furniture design as a branch of artistic creativity and learned to work in the novel materials he chose to employ so that the final product would be entirely his own creation.

Bugatti's first known furniture design was a bedroom suite created in 1880 to

celebrate the marriage of his sister to the painter Giovanni Segantini, and included two chairs in dark wood with motifs painted by Segantini himself. Although the ensemble was heavier than Bugatti's later work, the pseudo-Arabic wrought copper decoration and fretted details and the naturalistic painted motifs, influenced by Japonaiserie, were to become char-acteristic features. These influences are equally apparent in two chairs presented at the Italian exhibition of 1888 at Earl's Court, London — one of ebonised wood inlaid in white metal in a Mauresque style and the other with a Japanese floral design painted in brown and gold.

The peak of Bugatti's career, however, came with his designs of four rooms and

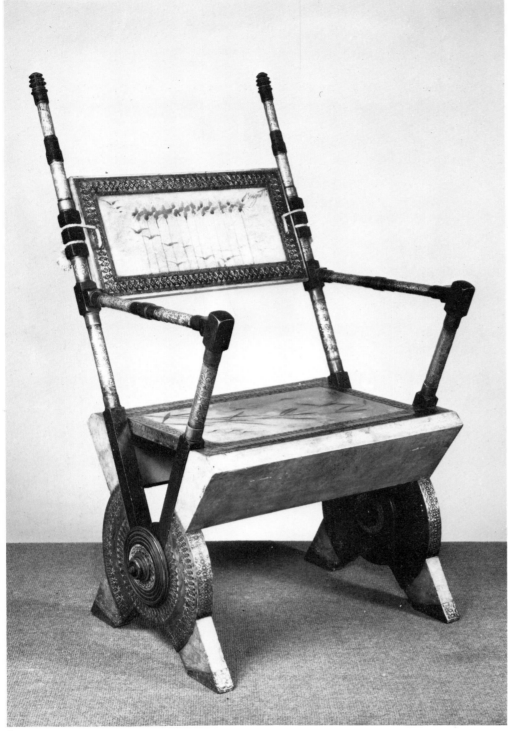

2

3

4

5

various individual items for the Turin exhibition of 1902. The chairs presented were the logical outcome of his work of the 1890s, which had shown a preference for sand-coloured vellum decorated with geometrical patterns based on stylised insect forms, with an increasing domination of the circle or part circle. At Turin, however, the wood of the furniture was completely covered in vellum, which disguised the joints and gave the illusion of furniture moulded in a plastic medium, while patterns based on stylised insects or pure geometry were boldly painted directly onto the vellum in gold and pastel shades, replacing the inlays of white and yellow metal, pale wood or ebony of his earlier work. Particularly notable were the 'G'

chairs of the 'snail' room, moulded in one sweeping curve with circular backs and seats, which provided an innovative and individual solution to the problem of contemporary seating in the space left at the back for tail-coats or trains to hang down unhampered.

While Bugatti's work is highly individual, certain elements such as the oriental inspiration, sculptural freedom and organic vigour of his designs, are nevertheless in keeping with the Art Nouveau trend. The range of his work, from the eclecticism of his early designs to the boldness of form and sophistication of detail of his work after 1900, shows an originality of conception which is matched only by the work of Antonio Gaudí.

1 Rocking chair, wood covered in yellow-tinted parchment decorated with coloured pencil.
2 Chair in walnut, painted vellum and repoussé brass, c.1900.
3 Bedroom created for the home of Lord Battersea, Surrey House, London, c.1900.
4 One of four rooms presented at the Turin exhibition of 1902.
5 The 'snail' room, with G-shaped chairs, presented at the Turin exhibition of 1902.

1

2

Antonio Gaudí i Cornet

1852-1926

The works of the Catalonian architect Antonio Gaudí i Cornet combine a rational approach to structure with a frenzied imaginative creativity, and are among the most original and bizarre of any period of architecture. Although his influence outside his native Catalonia was minimal during his lifetime, he has been recognised recently as one of the most inspired, if eccentric, innovators of the turn of the century.

Gaudí studied at the Barcelona School of Architecture from 1873 to 1878 before setting up his own practice in Barcelona, where he was to work for the rest of his lifetime. In the course of his career, his work — which consisted mainly of private houses for a few wealthy patrons

who shared his personal fervour for an independent Catalonia — developed from the early eclecticism of the Moorish Casa Vicens (1883-85) or Baroque Casa Calvet (1898) to the pure originality of the Casa Milá (1906-10), which is organic not only in decoration but also in form. After 1910, Gaudí renounced secular commissions to work on the Colonia Güell chapel and his most famous building, the Cathedral of the Sagrada Familia, which is still being built today.

Gaudí's chair designs represent imaginative sculptural solutions to the problems of structure, construction and materials. Although, as in the case of his architecture, their appearance is often unusual or bizarre, a closer examination

reveals both a thorough understanding of the traditional techniques of Catalonian craftsmen and a rational concern for 'fitness of purpose' — the pews in the Colonia Güell crypt, for example, were designed in such a way that conversation was made uncomfortable, and Gaudí also had the idea of making the column bases in the Sagrada Familia into seats which would be comfortable only when sitting upright.

Like his pews and church furniture, the chairs Gaudí designed for his secular commissions harmonise perfectly with their setting — the dining room of the Baroque Casa Calvet, for example, is furnished with an extravagant set of chairs covered in green silk and velvet, with carved legs of gilded wood. Although his most character-

3

4

5

istic and successful chairs are probably the simple, organically shaped pews, dining room or office chairs in carved oak, Gaudí also produced several *grand confort* designs for his houses, such as the richly upholstered chaise longue with wrought iron decoration in the Palau Güell (1898).

1   Dining chair created for the Casa Calvet, Barcelona 1898.
2   Oak side chair designed for the dining-room of the Casa Batlló, Barcelona 1905-07.
3   Giltwood sofa and chairs with silk upholstery, c.1900.
4   Dining-room of the Casa Batlló.
5   Interior of the crypt of the Colonia Güell chapel, Santa Coloma de Cervelló 1908-14.
6   Bench in the Park Güell, Barcelona 1900-14, with ceramic decoration by Josep Maria Jujol.

6

Opposite
1   BUGATTI Wood chair with vellum covered seat and back from a dining suite created for Bugatti's own use towards the end of his career.
2   BUGATTI Armchair of Moorish inspiration in wood and vellum with pierced copper decoration c.1895-1900.
3   GAUDI Pew in padouk wood and wrought iron from the crypt of the Colonia Güell chapel, Santa Coloma de Cervelló 1910. The back of the pew is set with an elbow rest for the use of those kneeling in the row behind.

Overleaf
ROUSSEAU Ebony and walnut chair with blue silk upholstery, 1921. The back is in tinted sharkskin with ivory inlay.

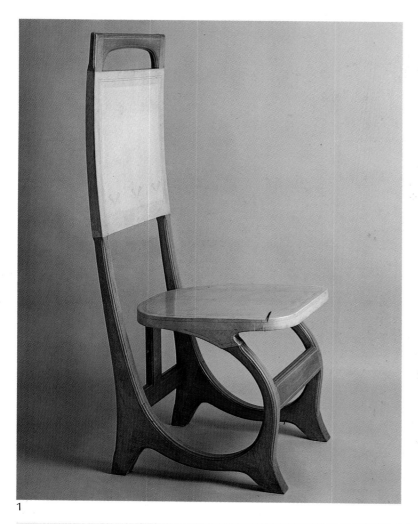

1

2

3

Art Deco

After the waning in the very early years of this century of the Art Nouveau movement, the next major stylistic manifestation was Art Deco, essentially a French style, the ingredients of which were already in the air before the hiatus of the First World War, and which emerged in its fully developed form in the early 1920s, finding its consummate expression in the French pavilions at the Paris exhibition of 1925. Art Deco was an essentially feminine style dependent on soft curves, restrained forms and formalised decoration in reaction to the sometimes excessive exuberance and vigour of Art Nouveau. The flourishes of Art Nouveau were replaced by a neo-classical restraint. A whole generation of designers emerged as the exponents of this new style and the chairs which many amongst them designed bear witness to the charm and appeal of the style and to the dominant role played by French designers in the applied arts. Art Deco can be seen as a defiant post-war manifestation of France's traditional supremacy since the eighteenth century as leader of taste and foremost in the standard of craftmanship.

The most important French ébéniste of the 1920s was Emile-Jacques Ruhlmann, responsible for several major schemes in the 1925 exhibition and for unusual and refined chair designs. Ruhlmann favoured the use of rich, heavily veined hardwoods such as Macassar ebony, with details such as sabots picked out in ivory. His chairs, indeed all his furniture, were the product of consummate craftsmanship, minutely painstaking and immensely costly. His version of Art Deco was simple, sometimes to the point of austerity. A characteristic feature of his chairs were the slender, fluted legs tapering into ivory sabots. The tapering fluted legs introduced by Ruhlmann were popularised in the less costly manufacture of chairs by such firms as Mercier Frères.

Maurice Dufrène and Jules Leleu were two amongst many to help spread Art Deco at a more popular level. The Compagnie des Arts Français of Louis Süe and André Mare produced distinctive Art Deco chairs in a slightly more bulbous style than that of Ruhlmann. Süe et Mare used highly polished richly coloured woods, often with deep upholstery in hide or velour. One of the prettiest rooms from the 1925 exhibition was the lady's bedroom by André Groult, which included a deep tub chair on bulbous feet, the structure covered in sharkskin, the upholstery of cut velvet.

Parallel with this richly decorative official style was another more avant-garde movement, equally concerned with luxury but drawing its inspiration through the fine arts from such sources as the arts of Central Africa. The influence of African art on the Cubist painters and the collecting of African artefacts in avant-garde artistic circles in Paris after 1905 is already well documented. Less well known is the work of that small, loose-knit group of furniture designers whose work was the direct product of this new influence. A central figure in this story was the couturier Jacques Doucet who, after selling off his collection of eighteenth-century furniture and works of art in 1912, set himself the task of collecting and commissioning the very best of contemporary art. He bought works of major Cubists, collected African art and patronised Eileen Gray, Pierre Legrain and Marcel Coard, Gustav Miklos, Rose Adler, Paul Iribe and Pierre Chareau. In the context of the chair, Pierre

CHAREAU Study of the Ambassade Française.   RUHLMANN Hôtel d'un Collectionneur.   DUNAND Smoking room Ambassade Française.

Legrain's contribution to Doucet's ensemble is particularly noteworthy. Using a wide variety of materials which included limed oak, palm wood, ivory, mother of pearl, sharkskin and lacquer, his designs for seat furniture included a stool based on an Ashanti model, a scoop-seated stool carved with geometric decoration, again based on a specific Central West African original, a bench seat inspired from a Mangbetu marriage stool and a rather clumsy chair which would seem to combine features of an Ashanti chief's chair with those of a Congolese royal Bojokwe chair. For another patron Legrain made a strongly Cubist chair in tobacco brown lacquer and vellum. His chair designs are a fascinating reflection of one of the major fine art influences of the twentieth century.

Eileen Gray was a highly individual designer whose most remarkable seat furniture design of the Art Deco period was the canoe-shaped day bed in lacquer for the Suzanne Talbot interior which she redecorated in the early 1920s. Lacquer, a material which she had started to use before the First World War, became very fashionable in the 1920s and found its greatest exponent in the person of Jean Dunand. This remarkable craftsman, capable of working on every scale from jewellery to entire rooms, brought a new sense of daring to the practice of the craft of lacquer, attempting large areas of undecorated lacquer and evolving decorating techniques that included the incrustation of minute particles of crushed eggshell or mother of pearl. Dunand made handsome lacquered chairs, simple, strong designs, often basic tub shapes raised on stepped legs. Particularly noteworthy was a cast concrete single-unit chair lacquered in black, made as a prototype in the 1930s but curiously anticipating in its sleek unified appearance the first single-unit plastic chairs made some twenty-five years later.

Perhaps the most important, if not the most immediately appreciated or influential chair to be made in the immediate post First World War period was the Dutchman Gerrit Rietveld's Red/Blue chair of 1918. The structure of this chair is technically simple to the point of banality, yet it achieves an extraordinary sophistication through its exploration of space and sense of visual lightness, especially in the all-black setting into which Rietveld finally put it. The chair is an intellectual resolution of a painterly quest towards the definition of space. It is also the proof, in Rietveld's words, that '. . . a thing of beauty, e.g. a spatial object, could be made of nothing but straight, machined materials'. With uniform square-sectioned lengths of wood and two rectangular planks Rietveld made a revolutionary chair. Perhaps, above all, he had made a chair that demanded discussion, a chair that opened up many new conceptual possibilities, a chair ahead of its time, produced, as it was, in an era still very much concerned with decoration. Other chairs of interest designed by Rietveld include an asymmetrical construction of 1923 and his minimal Zig-Zag of 1933, first put into production in 1934. It is the Red/Blue chair, however, that has entered history as the important precursor of the international Modern Movement which was to develop during the 1920s as a theoretical ideal, and emerge in the late 1920s and early 30s as a style for living in which space, light and emptiness were the key elements.

GROULT Lady's bedroom of the Ambassade Française.

GRAY Day bed in Suzanne Talbot's 'salon de verre', designed in 1933 by Paul Ruaud.

1

2

3

1   Wood chair with leather upholstery and brass capped feet, c.1922.
2   Upholstered armchair in metal and Macassar ebony, c.1927. In an article in *Art et Décoration,* Ruhlmann claimed that the idea of using metal in furniture design was a practical response to the problems posed by central heating, especially in the United States, which caused the wood to contract.
3   Chair with tapering legs executed from Ruhlmann's drawings of his preliminary project for the Hôtel d'un Collectionneur at the 1925 Paris exhibition. The black eggshell lacquer was done by Jean Dunand. Ruhlmann's original design was upholstered in leopardskin.

Emile-Jacques Ruhlmann

1879-1933

Like many of the best known designers of the 1920s, Emile-Jacques Ruhlmann was entirely self-taught. He was nevertheless highly successful, both as an interior designer and cabinet-maker, and at the end of the First World War was able to set up his own company, Etablissements Ruhlmann et Laurent, which soon became the most prestigious interior design company in Paris. Although he had exhibited at the Salon d'Automne in 1910 and 1913, the climax of his career came with the 1925 Paris exhibition, for which he designed the Hôtel d'un Collectionneur, in collaboration with a group of fellow artists, and the study of the Pavillon d'un Ambassadeur. He remained sensitive to changing tastes and fashions, and in the 1930s produced

work in chromium-plated metal and silver in a purist, modern style.

Ruhlmann is widely regarded as the greatest French ébeniste of the twentieth century, following in the grand tradition of the French eighteenth-century masters, and his furniture, with its emphasis on quality, formal and technical refinement and elegance, epitomises better than any other the neo-classical mode of Art Deco.

He believed that 'it is the élite which launches fashion and determines its direction', and the affluence of his clientele enabled him to experiment with exotic woods — purple amaranth, amboyna, Macassar ebony — and rich inlays of ivory, tortoiseshell, Moroccan leather or sharkskin. Ornament, however, was always

subordinated to the elegance and proportion of the whole, and Ruhlmann described his work as employing 'pure forms dictated by reason, beautiful proportion of volumes and elegance and directness of line', with inlays added as a finishing touch.

His chair designs use simple, at times monumental forms and are usually richly upholstered, with an emphasis on comfort. Their most distinctive characteristic is their finely tapered legs, often capped in ivory, which began to appear in his work after about 1913.

1

2

3

Süe et Mare and the Compagnie des Arts Français

The Compagnie des Arts Français was founded in 1919 by architect and painter Louis Süe (1875-1968) and painter André Mare (1887-1932) with the aim of uniting a team of artists of different disciplines who could collaborate on the design of complete interiors. Members of the group included the painter Bernard Boutet de Monvel, the tapestry designer and mural painter Gustave-Louis Jaulmes, the painter, sculptor and wood engraver Paul Véra, the glass worker Maurice Marinot and the graphic artist André Marty. Before its disbandment in 1928, Süe et Mare completed several interiors including the shop Parfums d'Orsay and the Pavillon Fontaine and Musée d'Art Contemporain at the Paris 1925 exhibition.

As a painter, Mare brought sensibility, spontaneity and a feeling for colour and decoration to the more rigorous architectural discipline of Süe, and together they created within the space of a decade a pure, cohesive French style which embraced every aspect of architecture and design. Formed partly in reaction to the 'monstrous dominance of a single personality' which characterised Art Nouveau, the Compagnie des Arts Français was less concerned with creating startling and fashionable interiors than with an adherence to the traditional values of sobriety and elegance. Their furniture was inspired by the period of Louis Philippe, and executed in rich, highly-polished woods with conventionalised floral Art

Deco motifs carved in low relief or inlaid in mother-of-pearl. Their chair designs encompass both large, comfortable, slightly bulbous upholstered models and side chairs in carved wood with flowing lines. Their contribution to the 1925 Exposition des Arts Décoratifs offered one of the best solutions to the French search for an identifiable style in the decorative arts, and constituted in itself a personal manifesto of the group's aims.

1, 3 Mahogany side chair with round seat and cabriole legs, c.1923. The seat and back are covered in brown leather or velvet.
2 Mahogany side chair with tapestry seat, c.1920-25. A companion armchair was also produced.

1

2

3

Eileen Gray

1879-1976

Eileen Gray was among the most inventive of the designers working in Paris between the two World Wars. Her work is characterised by an extreme originality of form and materials, in particular oriental lacquer.

Eileen Gray studied at the Slade School of Art in London from 1898, during which period she learned the technique of making oriental lacquer from a local craftsman, D. Charles. In 1902 she moved to Paris to study drawing at the Académie Colarossi and the Académie Julian. She continued her study of lacquer with Sugawara, a Japanese master who was to work with her into the 1920s, and by 1913 had exhibited examples of her work at the Salon de la Société des Artistes Décorateurs.

Eileen Gray spent the years of the First World War in London with Sugawara, and on her return to Paris in 1919 she received her most ambitious decorative commission — the rue de Lota apartment of Mme Mathieu Lévy, known professionally as the model Suzanne Talbot. By 1922 Gray was in a position to open her own gallery, Jean Désert, in the rue du Faubourg St.-Honoré, Paris to display and sell her furniture, lamps, mirrors and carpets, which she found economical to produce in small series of four and five. Although her principal interest was still lacquer work, it was her carpets, woven in her rue Visconti studio by apprentices supervised by Evelyn Wyld, which sold best.

In 1923, Gray created an ambitious display for the Salon des Artistes Décorateurs entitled a 'room-boudoir for Monte Carlo'. Although the French critics were unanimous in their contempt, her work received the acclaim of architects such as J. J. P. Oud and Walter Gropius, and she was encouraged to exhibit at the Salon d'Automne with Le Corbusier and Robert Mallet-Stevens. In 1924 she began to make architectural studies herself, and in 1927, in collaboration with Jean Badovici, designed E-1027 at Roquebrune. Gray closed Jean Désert in 1930 to concentrate on architecture, and her subsequent architectural works include a Paris apartment for Badovici (1930-31), the Tempe a Pailla, Castellar (1932-34) and several projects.

4

5

The career of Eileen Gray represents a perfect illustration of the transition from the exotic, individual craftsman-made objects of the early 1920s to the purposefully functional architecture and furniture of the Modern Movement. Her early work, exemplified in the interior for Mme Lévy, is characterised by unusual forms, often influenced by the current vogue for African art, and exotic materials and colours. The chairs in the rue de Lota apartment — salmon silk and orange armchairs, the former with arms carved to resemble the heads of rearing serpents, and a brown lacquered day-bed — were designed to compliment the genuine African objects and wild animal skins of Mme Lévy's collection, and the ensemble perfectly captures the luxury and eccentricity of 1920s Paris. In the designs for her own houses, however, Gray used harder, more geometrical forms, industrial materials and a more limited colour range. The functional simplicity of chairs such as the Transat chair of 1927, in black leather and chromed steel, is perfectly in keeping with the stark, Modernist interiors, and shows an acceptance of the new trends of the Modern Movement.

1 Patinated brown lacquer day-bed supported on twelve shallow arches, c.1919. Designed for the salon of Mme Lévy's rue de Lota apartment.

2 Transit chair: padded leather seat slung within a lacquer frame whose joints are expressed externally by the chromed steel connectors which also form a pivot for the back rest. Designed for the living room of E-1027, Roquebrune in 1927.
3 Folding hammock chair, painted laminated wood with suspended canvas upholstery, designed for the Tempe a Pailla, Castellar. The hammock chair can be folded in half for convenient storage.
4 Armchair in black leather with red lacquered arms carved to resemble serpents, c.1910-14. A version with salmon silk upholstery was used in Mme Lévy's rue de Lota apartment.
5 'Salon de verre' in Mme Lévy's apartment, designed by Paul Ruaud in 1933 using glass and white cellulose paint to create a Modernist setting for Gray's furniture.

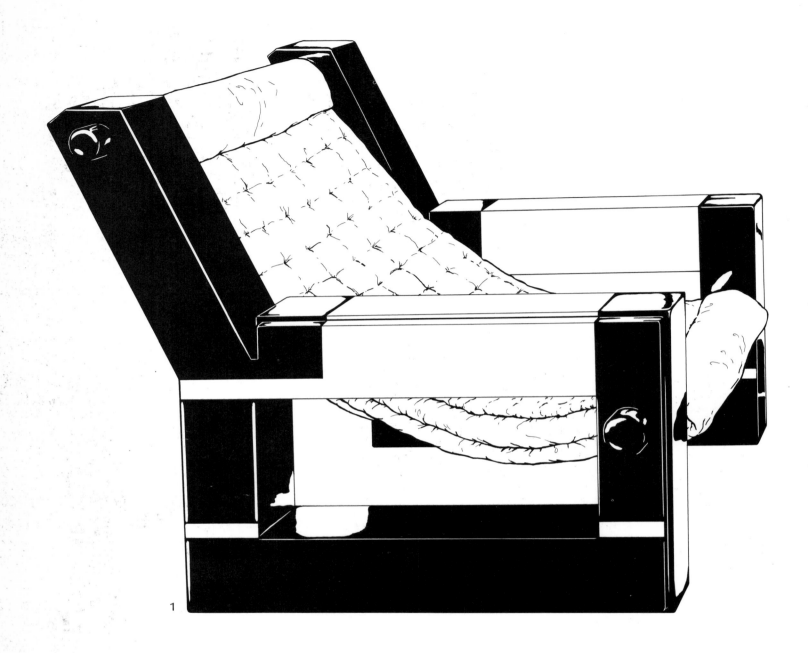

1

Pierre Legrain

1889-1929

Pierre Legrain studied at the Collège Sainte-Croix de Neuilly and at the Ecole des Arts Appliqués Germain Pilon. In 1908 he entered the studio of Paul Iribe with whom he worked until 1914, and he collaborated in the decoration of the couturier Jacques Doucet's apartment in the avenue du Bois. During this period he did some graphic design for the periodicals *Assiette au Beurre, La Baïonnette, Le Témoin* and *Le Mot,* and in 1917 Doucet offered him a salary to design book bindings and covers for new editions of contemporary authors. In 1919 Legrain left Doucet to work for René Kieffer and others, producing innovative designs for book bindings based on geometric forms and using unusual materials — mother-of-pearl, wood and sharkskin. He also continued his work as an interior designer, producing schemes for Mme J. Tachard, Pierre Meyer, Maurice Martin du Gard, and the Viscount of Noailles. In 1925 he was put in charge of the design of the interior of Doucet's villa at Neuilly, intended as a shrine to contemporary artistic achievement and a showcase for the work of Gray, Iribe, Groult, Coard, Modigliani, Matisse, Miró and Picasso.

Because of his lack of formal training as a cabinet-maker, Legrain found it easy to invent entirely new conceptions rather than merely modernising the traditional. Many of his remarkable chair designs, such as his Ashanti stool in sharkskin and lacquered wood, reflect the strong, agressive lines of the art of Central Africa. Their simple, rigid forms were executed in unusual textures and exotic materials — palmwood, Macassar ebony or limed oak with areas of gilt or coloured lacquer, polished chromium metal, ivory and sharkskin. He also produced more simple, elegant furniture in pale sycamore and chrome.

1   Armchair with slung seat, mahogany partially covered with vellum, c.1925.
2   African inspired chair in palmwood with vellum seat, c.1925-28, from the bathroom of Jacques Doucet's villa at Neuilly.
3   Armchair, wood with metal feet and leather upholstery, c.1930.

2

3

4

4   Bench of African inspiration, c.1922. The basic structure is in oak, stained black and treated with white lead, with side pieces of carved ebony. The inside and seat are lacquered in gold.

5, 6   Legrain's interpretation of an Ashanti stool in lacquered wood carved with gilded triangular motifs, together with the original.

7   'Siège curule', ebony with mother-of-pearl inlay, c.1923.

5

6

7

Paul Iribe

1883-1935

Paul Iribe played an important role in the emergent Art Deco style before the First World War, designing jewellery, fabrics, wallpapers, objets d'art, furniture and interiors. His 'rose Iribe', a highly conventionalised version of the flower inspired by Charles Rennie Mackintosh's rose motif, was widely imitated and became a key motif in the ornamental vocabulary of Art Deco. As an illustrator, Iribe contributed to *Assiette au Beurre,* founded the periodicals *Le Témoin* (1905) and *Le Mot,* and designed advertisements for lingerie and perfume for several publications including the *Gazette du Bon Ton.* During this period he also collaborated with Paul Poiret, both as fashion illustrator *(Les Robes de Paul Poiret),* and interior designer and in 1912 the

couturier Jacques Doucet commissioned him to furnish his own apartment in the avenue du Bois. Pierre Legrain worked in Iribe's studio from 1908 until 1914, when Iribe emigrated to America where he worked in theatre and cinema design with Cecil B. de Mille. He returned to France in 1930, and at the end of his life did some jewellery designs for Coco Chanel.

Like Emile-Jacques Ruhlmann, Iribe designed for an elite clientele. His chairs tend to be large and comfortable, based on elegantly curving lines. He favoured exotic materials such as amaranth, Brazilian rosewood, ebony and sharkskin, and his designs are characterised by a rich use of contrasting colours.

1   Swivel armchair with leopardskin upholstery and marquetry, c.1912-14.
2   Mahogany armchair with ebony inlay and mauve silk upholstery, 1913.

Clément Mère

1870-n.d.

Clément Mère studied painting in the studio of the academic painter Jean-Léon Gérôme in Paris. After a short period in his native Bayonne, he returned to Paris in 1900 where he joined the designers working for Julius Meier-Graefe's gallery and store La Maison Moderne. During this time he also collaborated with Franz Waldroff in the field of fashion design, making buttons, jewellery and small wooden and ivory boxes which they exhibited together from 1902. From 1910 Mère exhibited furniture at the Salon des Artistes Décorateurs and the Société Nationale.

Mère's chair designs are characterised by severe, often classical lines, with elaborate decoration using plaques of carved ivory, marquetry of exotic woods, panels of tooled leather and lacquer. His style includes intricate decoration based on insects, petals and shells.

1   Armchair in Macassar ebony and ivory with sides and back covered in repoussé leather.

Clément Rousseau

1872-n.d.

Clément Rousseau studied as a pupil of the sculptor Léon Morice. He first exhibited at the Salon des Artistes Français in 1920, and was amongst the group of avant-garde designers and decorators to be patronised in the early 1920s by the couturier Jacques Doucet.

Rousseau's chair designs display the classical lines and tapering legs of the work of Emile-Jacques Ruhlmann. He was one of the first, if not the first, designers to revive the use of sharkskin as a decorative inlay in furniture, with examples dating from before the First World War. He used sharkskin tinted in a variety of colours, usually in conjunction with dark woods and ivory, in designs which show both refinement and simplicity.

2   Ebony and walnut side chair with blue silk upholstery. The back is in tinted sharkskin with ivory inlay in a sunburst pattern, as shown in the colour illustration on page 92.

1

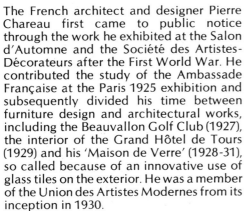
2

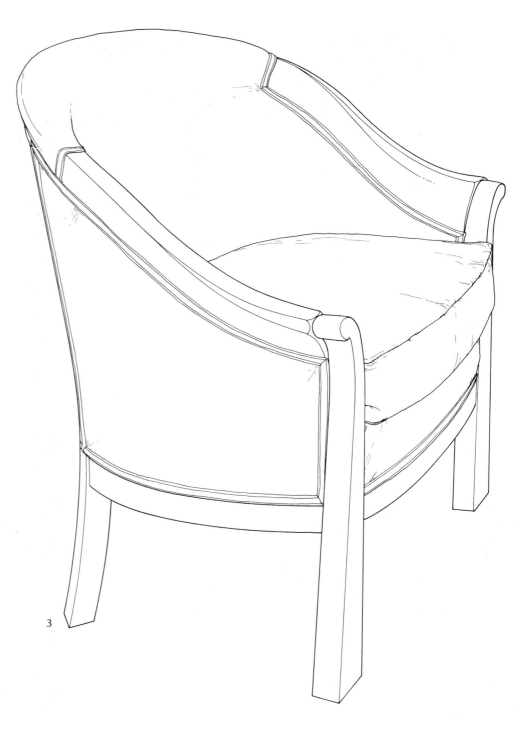
3

Pierre Chareau

1883-1950

The French architect and designer Pierre Chareau first came to public notice through the work he exhibited at the Salon d'Automne and the Société des Artistes-Décorateurs after the First World War. He contributed the study of the Ambassade Française at the Paris 1925 exhibition and subsequently divided his time between furniture design and architectural works, including the Beauvallon Golf Club (1927), the interior of the Grand Hôtel de Tours (1929) and his 'Maison de Verre' (1928-31), so called because of an innovative use of glass tiles on the exterior. He was a member of the Union des Artistes Modernes from its inception in 1930.

Chareau's furniture was usually designed for the interiors of his own com-

missions. His chair designs of the early 1920s show a preference for undecorated ample rounded forms, executed in highly polished woods — mahogany, walnut, oak, ash or maple — with rich upholstery. Later in the decade he began to experiment with furniture using metal frames for public commissions such as bars, hotels, and clubs. His designs for chairs, stools, tables and cupboards in wood and metal received much praise from contemporary publications for their functional approach and combination of elegance and technical ingenuity. Chareau often retained the industrial character of the frame by painting it matt black in preference to the highly polished steel favoured by most of his contemporaries.

1   Reading room in the Grand Hôtel, Tours 1928.
2   Bar and smoking room in the Grand Hôtel, Tours.
3   Light wood armchair with grey buckskin upholstery, 1925.

1

2

3

Robert Mallet-Stevens

1886-1945

The architect and designer Robert Mallet-Stevens was one of the first French artists to recognise that the traditional French virtues of high quality craftsmanship and 'artistic' taste could no longer compete with the 'modern' qualities of Austrian and German design, introduced to France through the exhibition by a group of Munich artists at the Salon d'Automne in 1910. By 1913, in his 'salon de musique' exhibited at the Salon d'Automne, he had introduced a style based on clear lines and geometrical forms which was to be the basis of his Parisian houses and department stores of the 1920s and 1930s. His work for the Paris exhibition of 1925 — a winter garden for the Habitation Moderne, the entrance hall of the Ambassade Française

and the Pavillon de Tourisme, with its simple, cubic form and reinforced concrete tower — showed the functional simplicity which was to characterise French avant-garde architecture of the late 1920s and early 1930s.

In 1930 Mallet-Stevens became the first president of the Union des Artistes Modernes, a group of architects and designers united in their opposition to the rejection of new materials and reliance on expensive, hand-made furniture of the Société des Artistes-Décorateurs. Like his fellow members, Mallet-Stevens believed that the interior of the future should be suited to the needs of contemporary life, with functional simplicity as its major criterion. His chair designs are usually in

tubular steel, sometimes upholstered in fabrics of cubist inspiration, and are characterised by simple lines and sombre colours. Although made originally for his own architectural commissions, they were designed with the possibility of economical mass-production in mind.

1   High stool, tubular steel painted dark brown with golden brown leather seat, from Mallet-Stevens' study in his Auteuil house.
2   Hall, presented at the Salon des Artistes Décorateurs, 1928.
3   Armchair, tubular steel painted dark brown with golden brown leather seat. Part of the furnishings of Mallet-Stevens' study in his Auteuil house.

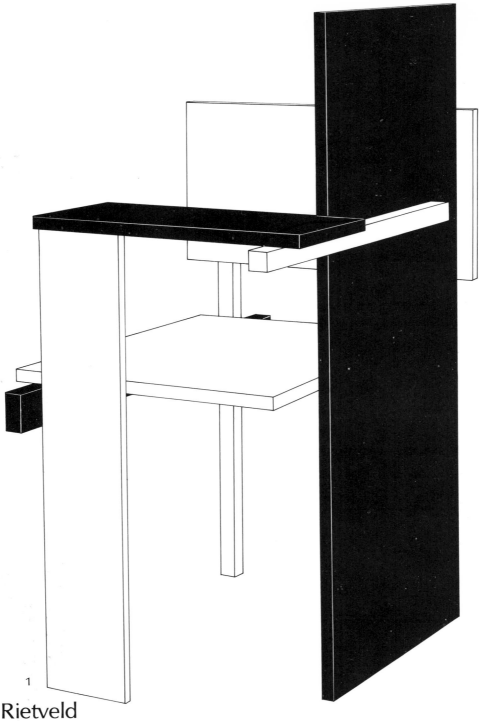

1

Gerrit Thomas Rietveld

1888-1964

The Dutch architect and designer Gerrit Thomas Rietveld left school at the age of eleven to enter his father's cabinet-making workshop. He then served an apprenticeship with the jeweller C. J. Begeer before opening his own cabinet-making workshop and retailers in Utrecht in 1911. During this period Rietveld studied architecture at night school under P. J. C. Klaarhamer, whose work was to provide inspiration for his furniture designs. He joined the De Stijl group in 1918, and in 1924 designed the Schröder House, Utrecht, which was a perfect concrete expression of the group's architectural principles. During the early 1930s Rietveld received several commissions for houses, shops and a cinema. His later works, following a revival

of interest in De Stijl in the 1950s, include the Stoop House, Velp (1951), the Soonsbeek sculpture pavilion near Arnhem (1954) and the Ploeg textile factory, Bergeyk (1956).

Although Rietveld began to design chairs in about 1900 his first important design, the Red/Blue chair, was not produced until 1918. Described by van Doesburg as an 'abstract-real sculpture', the Red/Blue chair 'was created with the intention of demonstrating that an aesthetic and spatial object could be constructed with linear material and made by machinery'. Its severe, right-angled geometry and use of primary colours make it a perfect embodiment of the principles of De Stijl painters — an aesthetic which

Rietveld was to develop further in designs such as the Berlin chair of 1923 and the 'Military series' of 1923-25.

In 1927 Rietveld produced his first designs using tubular steel — the Beugel-fauteuil and Beugelstoel — which have curved plywood seats supported by continuous lengths of chrome metal tubing. In the same year he also created his first 'single-sheet' design — a chair for Dr. W. Birza made of a single sheet of fibre board which was cut with a jig-saw and then folded and glued into a structurally rigid form.

By 1934, Rietveld's search for a reductive simplicity had reached its peak in the Zig-Zag chair, an interpretation of the cantilever principle in wood using bolted

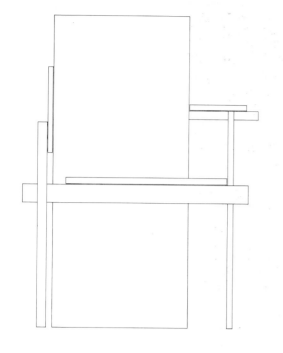

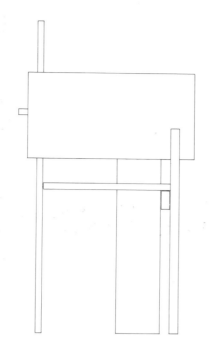

3

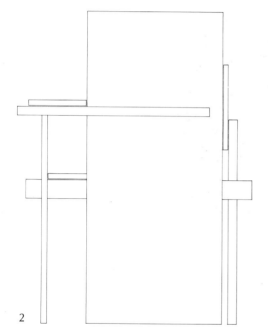

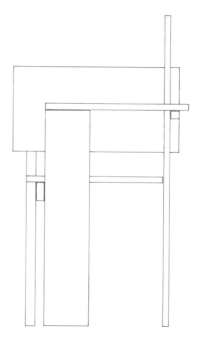

4

2

5

triangular joints to maintain rigidity. His 'crate' furniture of the same year, executed in the untreated red spruce usually reserved for packing cases and sold in kit form to be assembled at home by the purchaser, was a response to the economic crisis of the 1930s, and put useful, inexpensive seating using basic structures and cheap materials within the reach of a vast public.

Throughout his career, Rietveld continued to experiment with unusual materials and techniques, and his designs include a series of armchairs ranging from the single-sheet aluminium chair of 1942 to the Unesco chair of 1958, entirely upholstered in foam rubber. Rietveld drew his inspiration directly from the material, in

the manner of a sculptor, rather than drawing up plans at a drawing board. His designs typically combine aesthetic considerations with a desire to fully exploit the advantages of particular materials for economical machine production.

1   Berlin chair, 1923, deal lacquered black, slate grey and light grey. Designed for the Dutch pavilion at the Berlin exhibition.

2   Berlin chair, front, side, back and side elevations.
3   Beugelfauteuil, 1927, chrome metal tubing frame with curved plywood seat and back lacquered black or white. The armchair, together with two chairs of similar structure without arms designed in 1928, was put into production by Metz & Co. (Amsterdam and The Hague) in 1930.
4   Crate chair, 1934, untreated red spruce lacquered in colours chosen by the client and produced by Metz & Co. Rietveld's crate furniture is now manufactured in deal by Cassina.
5   Single-sheet aluminium chair, 1942. Designed during the Second World War, the aluminium chair was possibly inspired by pilot's seats and shows Rietveld's willingness to experiment with available materials and economical means of production.

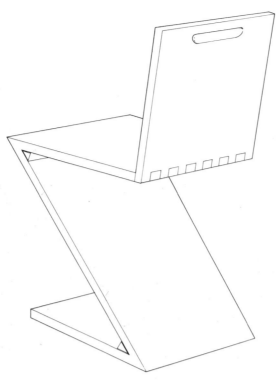

6   Zig-Zag chair, 1934, front elevation and perspective. The Zig-Zag chair, made of untreated elmwood, was originally executed by G. van de Groenekan, and manufactured after 1935 by Metz & Co. Versions lacquered red or green with white edging were used by Rietveld in his country houses of 1938-42, and versions with arms and a child's chair also exist.
7   Red/Blue chair, 1918, and Zig-Zag chair, 1934.

Opposite
Red/Blue chair, 1918, perspective and side and front elevations. A first unpainted version of the chair was made in oak with larger dimensions in 1917-18. This version, designed after Rietveld became a member of the De Stijl group, is in deal with ebony aniline dye, with the back, seat and terminals lacquered red, blue and yellow. The Red/Blue chair was manufactured originally by G. van de Groenekan, and since 1971 by Cassina.

Overleaf
1   MICHAEL GRAVES Alexander House extension, Princeton, 1971. Sitting room, with basculant and chaise longue by Le Corbusier.
2   MICHAEL GRAVES Alexander House extension. Library, with basculants by Le Corbusier.

6

7

1

Modern Movement

The International Style, or 'Modernist' Movement had its roots in the Netherlands, in the group which included Rietveld and came to be known as the 'De Stijl' group; in Paris, where Le Corbusier was the strongest influence, making his presence felt at the Paris 1925 exhibition with his Pavillon de l'Esprit Nouveau; but above all in Germany in the theories and achievements of the designers of the Bauhaus school.

The motivation behind the Bauhaus output of chair designs was complex, distilling the theorising of three-quarters of a century into a highly fertile few years of creativity. The results are characterised above all by a self-conscious functionalism, a paring down to essentials in keeping with the demands of industrialised production, and a strong emphasis on new materials, in particular chromium-plated steel, the visual appeal of which evoked directly the marriage of design and technology. Within the story of Bauhaus chair design two names emerge as chair designers of central importance — architect/designers Marcel Breuer and Ludwig Mies van der Rohe.

Breuer was responsible for the first chair to be constructed in chromium-plated tubular steel. Inspired, apparently, by the chromium-plated tubular structure of a cycle handlebar, Breuer created the complex 'Wassily' chair in 1925 as part of the furnishings of the Bauhaus campus home of his friend the painter Wassily Kandinsky. The chair is constructed around a basic framework of a single continuous line of tubing within which are cleverly slung intersecting planes of canvas or hide to form seat, back and arms. The exploration of space by this somewhat elaborately contrived interplay of surfaces and lines marks the 'Wassily' as the direct descendent of Rietveld's Red/Blue chair which was exhibited at the Bauhaus in 1923 and clearly influenced Breuer, then still a student. Although he was to design other chairs, both elegant and functional, it is for the 'Wassily' that Breuer is most acclaimed. He is said to have been the first to put forward the idea for the cantilever tubular steel chair but it was not until 1928 that he designed his own cantilever, his 'Cesca', after the idea had already been put into effect by others. Credit for the first cantilever chair must go to the Dutch architect/designer Mart Stam who, working independently, created a chair on this principle in 1926. Lightness and mobility were important to Stam and this chair was seen as a perfect solution. One of the most interesting designs by Breuer from his Berlin period, before his move to London in 1935, was a chair constructed in aluminium, Breuer's entry for a competition of aluminium furniture designs to be held in Paris.

Mies van der Rohe, Breuer's senior by about fifteen years, emerges as the more important chair designer. Although Stam had designed the first cantilever, Mies claimed the first successful exploitation of the principle as his own. He argued that the stability of Stam's design depended on the presence of solid bars within the angles of the tubular steel, thus eliminating the essential natural springiness and resilience of the concept. Mies maintained that he '. . . was the first to have exploited consistently the spring qualities of steel tubes'. The result was the M R chair, a far more

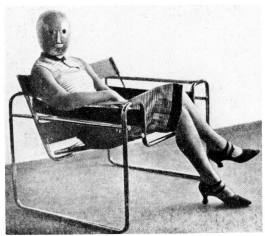

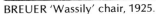

BREUER 'Wassily' chair, 1925.   LE CORBUSIER Grand confort, 1928.   MIES VAN DER ROHE Barcelona chair, 1929.

elegant design than Stam's, and in which the tension, rather than being concentrated at emphatic angles, was spread through the length of a stylish curve. This chair, with the seating in either cane or leather and with optional arms, was exhibited at the Stuttgart Werkbund and in the Mode der Dame exhibition in Berlin in 1927. Mies was granted his patent and was to derive a substantial part of his income from his technical resolution of a possibility first perceived by others. Constructed in steel tubing with a wall thickness of only two millimetres, Mies' cantilever designs, of which he was to produce quite a range during the early 1930s, combine functionalism, elegance, a visual and actual lightness and the natural resilience which is the true basis of the architectural cantilever principle. In 1931 he designed an elegant upholstered lounge chair with optional arms and in the same year an inviting chaise longue, similarly upholstered. He sketched endless variants which were never put into production, but the sketches in themselves are fascinating in their revelation of his thought process, his energy and patience in pursuit of perfection of proportions and details. Before progressing to his designs in flat steel, it is difficult to overlook the understated refinement of his wood-framed, leather-covered couch of 1930 on its four short legs of tubular steel, a truly patrician concept in seat furniture.

If Mies was master of tubular steel, he proved himself equally able in the design of chairs in flat steel. His most important was the Barcelona chair and ottoman of 1929, created for the German pavilion at the Barcelona International Exhibition of that year. The chair was specifically conceived as a royal seat, for the use of Alfonso XIII and his Queen during the opening ceremonies, and it is imbued with an aristocratic sense of occasion which makes it more appropriate perhaps to prestigious public settings than to domestic use. The basic 'X' structure, drawn in curves of a seemingly effortless refinement which belie the meticulous precision of Mies' design, has its origins in the folding stools of ancient Egypt or the curule chairs of ancient Rome. Although the cost of labour has today made all Mies' tubular designs relatively far more expensive, contradicting their original intention as inexpensive ideas for mass-production, the Barcelona has always been an expensive chair to produce and is unashamedly, though unostentatiously aristocratic. The comparable Tugendhat chair of 1929-30 is a less satisfying design. Another interesting comparison exists in the Brno chair, first conceived in tubular steel in 1929-30 but subsequently produced in flat steel, the latter undoubtedly the more pleasing design.

In France the first expression of Modernism was in the Pavillon de l'Esprit Nouveau at the 1925 exhibition, a hint of the future within an exhibition which was for the most part retrospective. It is perhaps surprising that some of the very earliest Modernist seat furniture designed in France was the work of Eileen Gray, an artist who, during the 1910s and early 20s had been so deeply involved in luxury and decoration as ends in themselves. Joseph Rykwert, re-appraising her importance as a pioneer of design in a 1972 article in the *Architectural Review,* pin-points designs for seat furniture in tubular steel executed in 1925, the same year as Breuer's 'Wassily' chair. During the late 1920s

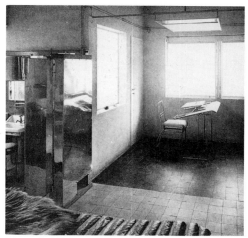
GRAY E-1027, Roquebrune, 1926-9.

CHAREAU Louis Sognot bar, c.1927.

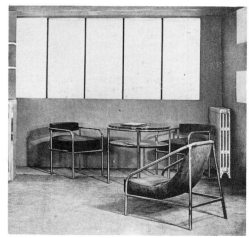
HERBST Dining-room, c.1928.

and 30s Miss Gray was to produce many highly individual Modernist chairs, often only in roughly-made prototype. Her most successful designs include the well-upholstered deep tub chair on a chromed tubular metal base first created between 1927 and 1929 for her house at Roquebrune, the production of which has only recently been resumed by Aram Designs; her Transat chair in which the upholstered seat is slung in a slender knock-down frame of bare or lacquered wood and chromed metal joints; and a curious folding hammock chair in laminated wood created in the late 1930s for her house at Castellar.

The French designers working in the Modernist style grouped themselves into the Union des Artistes Modernes (U.A.M.), holding their first exhibition in 1930. The founding committee included René Herbst and Robert Mallet-Stevens, both of whom contributed interesting, though unexceptional variants on the tubular metal chair. Pierre Chareau, who had been involved in the decoration of Doucet's villa, developed an individual style in the Modernist ethic, often combining wood with strips and rods of wrought iron, notably in unusual desks and stools. Perhaps his most exciting project was the 'Maison de Verre' created between 1928 and 1931 for a Dr Dalsace. Chareau was allowed a free rein and incorporated a variety of seat furniture including a tubular metal day bed.

The most important Modernist chair designer in France, however, was undoubtedly Charles Edouard Jeanneret, known as Le Corbusier. A spirited advocate of Modernism, Le Corbusier created a range of chairs that express his ideals with great sophistication. The best known and most successful is his chaise longue of 1928, designed for the furnishing of a villa in the Ville d'Avray and first exhibited at the Salon d'Automne in 1929. The seat frame of chromium-plated steel is adjustable for angle on the black mild steel base. The sleek ponyskin covering adds to the tactile appeal. In an article published in *The Studio* in April 1929, Le Corbusier's colleague Charlotte Perriand expressed their pursuit of a new aesthetic: 'METAL plays the same part in furniture as cement has done in architecture. IT IS A REVOLUTION. If we use metal in conjunction with leather for chairs . . . we get a range of wonderful combinations and new aesthetic effects.' And she talks of 'a new lyric beauty, regenerated by mathematical science'. In collaboration with Perriand and Pierre Jeanneret and for the same villa, Le Corbusier created his basculant, best described as a less complex version of the 'Wassily' and his grand confort, the latter effectively a basket of tubular metal into which are slotted the hide cushions that form the seat, back and arms. In this design, Le Corbusier quite literally turned inside out the tradition of the upholstered armchair.

In England chair design in the Modernist ethic found its strongest advocates in the artists of the Isokon group, and its greatest commercial success in the production of Pel or Practical Equipment Limited. The firm of Isokon was founded in December 1931. The key figures involved were Jack Pritchard and the architect Wells Coates and, a few years later, a self-exiled Marcel Breuer. The trade name was an abbreviation of the term 'Isometric Unit Construction', and

SUMMERS Plywood armchair, c.1930.

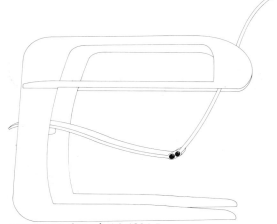

WEBER 'Airline chair', 1934-5.

expressed the group's ideal of modern functional design. Isokon produced new ideas in ply and laminated woods, sometimes buying models by outside designers. Their most celebrated design is the chaise longue designed in ply and laminate by Breuer. Contractual arrangements for its manufacture were first discussed in 1935 though the final design was not completed until spring 1936. The chair is well described in a contemporary sales leaflet 'The Isokon Long Chair is shaped to the human body. It fits you everywhere . . . These chairs have all the beauty of right design. Their lines express ease, comfort and well-being.' The designer Gerald Summers, working for the firm Makers of Simple Furniture conceived a clever and unusual plywood armchair cut out and shaped from a single rectangular sheet.

Tubular steel furniture was introduced into England by Serge Chermayeff, appointed head of the Modern Art Studios of Waring and Gillow in 1928. In that year he introduced the British public, notably, to the designs of the Bauhaus. Cold steel was generally deemed too austere for domestic use but ideal for contract furnishing. Pel, an offspring of Accles and Pollock, first established in 1929 and christened in 1932, filled this need admirably with a wide range of essentially plagiarised styles, the most useful of which were the stacking chairs so admirably suited to institutional use.

In the United States Modernism manifested itself in a distinctly American mode, the keynote of which was an obsession with streamlining. This more plastic, more fluid interpretation of the International Modern style became a strong influence on the styles of the 1950s. It was a less harsh style than its, at times, cold European counterpart, although many American designers worked in a style indistinguishable from that prevalent in Europe. A design such as Kem Weber's 'Airline Chair' of 1934-5, however, has a sculptured silhouette that is distinctly American.

The 1930s saw the creation of an interesting range of chairs by the Finnish architect Alvar Aalto. He made a speciality of work in ply and laminated woods and achieved his first success with his armchair 41, used in the TB Sanatorium at Paimio and subsequently manufactured by Artek. The chair was the product of three years of experiment and its virtues were well described in the *Architectural Review* in August 1933. 'This is the first pliant chair built without a rigid or semi-rigid framework: the construction lying not in the stouter plywood of the "wheels" . . . but in the interior bending tensions of the material forming the seat-back . . . Though buoyant as a spring-cushion the seat-back is virtually unbreakable . . . It is impossible to imagine a more comfortable chair, though it will ultimately be the cheapest.' Aalto's other best known design was the product of his application of the cantilever principle to the creation of a chair in wood rather than metal. His chair 31, first used in the furnishing of the Viipuri Library in 1933 and subsequently mass-produced by Artek, exploits the natural resilience of the laminated wood.

The International Modern style chair paved the way for post-war developments in a process of natural evolution. Certain elements amongst the avant-garde, however, and in particular certain Parisian decorators, became bored with the simplicity and the essential seriousness of the

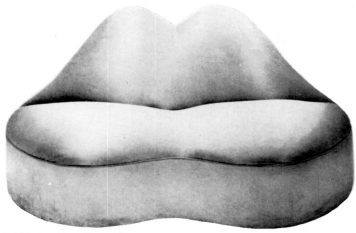

DALI Mae West lips sofa, c.1936.

BRITISH ARMY Pneumatic chaise longue.

Modernist chair and the 1930s saw a neo-Baroque revival in decoration. This combined with the new vogue for Surrealism to inspire a number of remarkable chairs, the sheer eccentricity of which injected a note of humour into what was becoming an altogether too serious subject. Salvador Dali, the ultimate *agent provocateur,* and creator of the extraordinary sofa in the form of Mae West's lips, wrote amusingly that 'People were constantly asking me, "What does that mean?" One day I received a present from my very good friend Jean-Michel Frank, the decorator; two chairs in the purest 1900 style. I immediately transformed one of them . . . I changed its leather seat for one made of chocolate. Then I had a golden Louis XV door-knob screwed under one of the feet . . . making the chair lean far over . . . and giving it an unstable balance so calculated that it was only necessary to walk heavily or bang the door to make the chair topple over. One of the legs was to repose continuously in a glass of beer which also would spill each time the chair keeled over. I called this dreadfully uncomfortable chair, which produced a profound uneasiness in all who saw it, the "atmospheric chair". And what does that mean, eh?' Clearly there was more to chair design than an ergonomic ideal. Humour and novelty had their part to play. Not until the 'Pop' furniture of the late 1960s was there to be a comparable injection of humour into the history of the chair.

The 1930s closed with the outbreak of war, with the result that the 1940s became difficult years in Europe for the production of anything other than goods essential to the war effort. In England after November 1942 all furniture manufacturers were obliged to conform to the limitations of Utility furniture, the specifications for which were laid down under the artistic direction of Gordon Russell. Utility chairs are a sad reflection of their time. The positive contribution to chair design emerging from the circumstances of the war was in the exploration of new materials including lightweight alloys developed for the aircraft industry and new synthetic materials. The BA chair designed by Ernest Race in 1945 was an elegant solution to the problem of using available materials. Its slender frame was cast from re-smelted scrap aluminium alloy. First shown at the 'Britain Can Make It' exhibition of 1946 the chair went on to win a gold medal at the Milan Triennale in 1951. Over a quarter of a million copies of his chair were manufactured. The 'Britain Can Make It' exhibition included another chair that was a direct product of the war, yet curiously prophetic — the pneumatic chaise longue developed from war-time inflatable craft was the precursor of the transparent P.V.C. chairs that were to enjoy a brief success in the late 1960s.

The post-war style of chair was characterised by the separate treatment of body and legs with the pursuit of single-unit organic forms for the seat, which would then be set on slender metal or tapering pale wood legs. How typically post-war in every respect is this brief caption to a chair designed by Dennis Lennon and illustrated in the *Studio Year Book* of 1950-51. 'Very lightweight easy chair, aluminium shell on a mahogany frame, with Dunlopillo padding and upholstery in rayon'. One of the most interesting British designs was Dennis Young's Shell chair, created in the late 1940s and featured in the Festival of Britain Exhibition in 1951. The anthropomorphic forms of

LATIMER Armchair 1951.

KEITH 'Intruder' sofa 1949.

SPENCE 'Allegro' chair, 1949.

the seat unit were heat moulded from Fibrenyle, a new thermoplastic material. The separate steel rod legs and substructure could be simply bolted into position. This idea of the enveloping chair can be seen in the post-war style of wing armchair popularised by designers such as Howard B. Keith who produced a series of variants on the theme including his 'Cavalier' and 'Intruder' of 1949. Keith was one amongst a new generation of furniture designers whose work became more widely known after its exposure at the Festival of Britain. The new group included Basil Spence, Robin Day and Clive Latimer and Lucian Ercolani, whose variants on such traditional British chairs as the Windsor have in themselves become classics. Geoffrey Dunn of Dunn's of Bromley was at the forefront as a creator and retailer of the new style chair and furnishings.

In France the U.A.M., established as the promoters of Modernism, now encouraged this new, more organic style. For the origins of the post-war style of chair, which one should perhaps dub 'Organic Modernist', one must look, however, to the United States, to the soft, sculptured Streamlined Modern of the 1930s and, perhaps most significantly, to a competition for 'Organic Design in Home Furnishings' organised by the Museum of Modern Art in 1940.

The competition was sponsored by retailers and manufacturers as a means of encouraging originality in American design. There followed an exhibition at the Museum in 1941 where considerable attention was drawn to the innovative work of two designers whose joint entries of designs for seating and other living room furniture had won them first prize. The two men were Eero Saarinen and Charles Eames, the former the son of the architect and director of the Cranbrook Academy of Art, Eliel Saarinen, the latter an architect and fellow of the Cranbrook Academy.

Theirs was a revolutionary approach to chair design. At the basis of their designs were shells of shaped plywood, but they went one stage further than Aalto, whose plywood was only ever curved in one direction. Saarinen and Eames pressed the ply into complex multi-directional curves giving a new shade of meaning to the organisers' concept of 'organic', for the term had been intended to signify a sense of wholeness, of unity within a decorative scheme. Saarinen and Eames' designs were organic in every sense. The soft silhouettes of their chairs allowed for considerable fluidity within the arrangement of a room whilst the shapes themselves were of a curvilinear freedom that seemed to combine the ideal of French or Belgian abstract-organic Art Nouveau with the essential simplicity of Modernism. Amongst the most interesting designs submitted by this team was a lounging chair of asymmetrical form, the upholstered shell, reminiscent of an amoeba or a sculpture by Arp, raised on four steel rod legs, and a relaxation chair, similarly conceived as a monocoq on steel rod legs. The ply shell is very cleverly conceived as an enveloping series of curves with an oval cut out at the base of the back. This cut-out detail gives a flexibility to what would otherwise have been a non-resilient scoop, for the entire back can now spring from the arms. This principle was in evidence again in an experimental chair of 1944 by Eames conceived as a series of overlapping units of moulded plywood. In this prototype was the basis of his most celebrated chair

EAMES Experimental lounge chair, c.1944.　　　WEGNER 'Chinese' chair, 1944.　　　JACOBSEN 'Swan' chair, 1958.

design, the classic 1956 lounge chair and ottoman.

The 1940-1 relaxation chair was possibly the inspiration for Dennis Young's Shell chair, the silhouette of which bears an uncanny resemblance to Eames' original. During the 1940s Eames applied himself to seemingly endless variations on the basic types which he had introduced, notably his dining or side chairs with separate moulded ply seat and back on steel or ply legs. From 1950 dates his moulded polyester armchair on its criss-cross wire base or rod legs. Perhaps his most extraordinary design, however, was the eccentric prototype lounging chair of 1948. The asymmetrical shell of hard rubber between two layers of plastic was a remarkable sculptural experiment. Eames was a chair designer who combined imagination with an architect's concern for detail.

Eames piloted a new era of chair design in America during the 1940s. In Europe, however, the most exciting innovations were to come from the Scandinavian countries and from Italy. From Scandinavia came a new interpretation of the traditional hand-crafted wooden chair, the result of a revival of interest in the natural beauties of wood. Hans Wegner, the Danish designer, was a typical exponent of this trend with such designs as his cherrywood 'Chinese' chair of 1944 and his definitive statement 'The chair' of 1949. One of the most adventurous of the Scandinavian designers was the Dane Arne Jacobsen, though it was not until the 1950s that he produced his sculptural, novel designs such as the 'Swan' chair (1958).

From Italy came new shapes and ideas in construction. The most noteworthy chair designer was Carlo Mollino, whose products would seem to be truly the creations of a frustrated sculptor with their strong boomerang shapes, anthropomorphically formed seats or backs and Arp-like volumes. For the two firms of Appelli and Varesio, and Cellerino, Mollino made remarkable chairs which have not, as yet, enjoyed the full reappraisal they deserve. Another master of the new Italian school was Carlo Enrico Rava, whose chairs are characterised by slender, eccentrically curved limbs. Osvaldo Borsani designed adjustable sofas and chaises longues for Tecno of Milan.

From the Great Exhibition to the excited mood of post-war Italian design, the chair has undergone seemingly endless changes. It has been far more than a merely utilitarian item of furniture, for within the story of chair design is the chronicle of a full century of changing fashions and influences. The chair has become a symbolic illustration, not only of progress in the specialised field of design history, but often of the broader aspects of social and economic history and of technological progress.

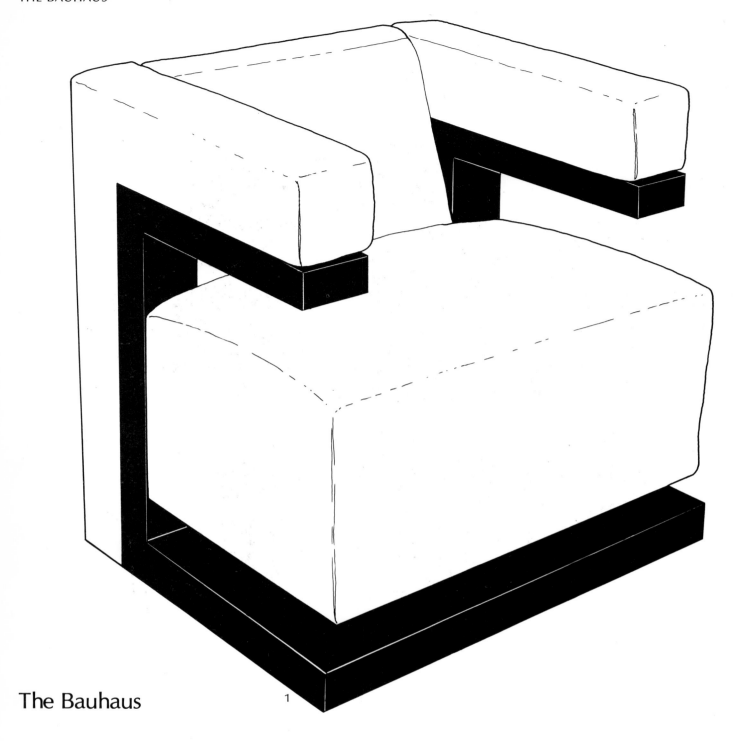

1

The Bauhaus

The 'Staatliches Bauhaus in Weimar' was a school of building, design and craftsmanship founded in 1919 by Walter Gropius from the amalgamation of two existing Weimar schools — the School of Arts and Crafts and the Academy of Fine Arts. Gropius's aim was to create 'a new guild of craftsmen, without the class distinctions which raise a barrier between craftsman and artist' who could conceive of building as a collective effort in which each artist-craftsman would contribute his part with a full awareness of its purpose in relation to the whole. His radical teaching programme consisted of two parallel courses — one devoted to the study of materials and crafts and the other to the theories of form and design. Students were given a preliminary course involving analyses of colour, form, materials, textures and rhythms together with training in several media to reveal their natural aptitudes. This was followed by workshops in several subjects including architecture, sculpture, painting, photography, metal, carpentry, ceramics, stained-glass and stage design.

Throughout its history the Bauhaus was plagued by political opposition, and in 1925 the school was forced to move to Dessau by the local Thuringian Government. In 1928 Hannes Meyer replaced Gropius as director, but in 1930 he was forced to resign by the Lord Mayor of Dessau in favour of Mies van der Rohe. The Dessau city council decided to dissolve the Bauhaus in 1932 and Mies' attempt to continue as a private institute in Berlin was finally thwarted in 1933 when the building was surrounded and searched by the police, and thirty-two students arrested.

Between 1919 and 1928 Gropius succeeded in forming a school and movement from a diverse collection of individualists including Wassily Kandinsky, Paul Klee, Johannes Itten, Marcel Breuer and Laszlo Moholy-Nagy. In the early days, carpentry was taught by Johannes Itten (1921-22), Walter Gropius (1922-25), Joseph Zachmann (1921-22) and Reinhold Weidensee (1922-25). The turning point, however, came in 1925 when Marcel Breuer was put in charge of the interiors workshop and inspired his pupils to produce the simple, functional furniture in tubular steel and

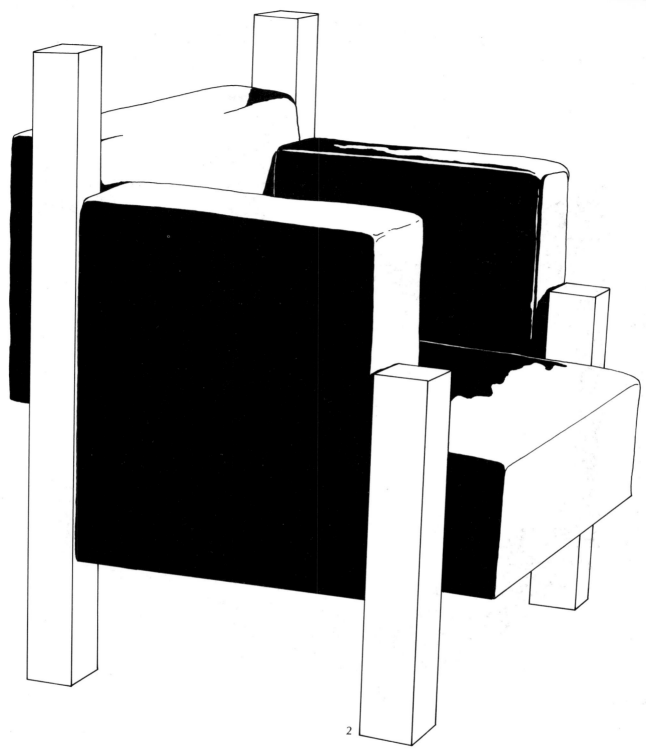

2

wood for which the school became known.

In 1928 Breuer was replaced by Josef Albers, and work was concentrated on experiments with bentwood, in particular folding chairs of bentwood and tubular steel. Under the supervision of Alfred Arndt (1929-1932), these experiments were taken even further in the direction of design anonymity, for Arndt believed that because of the current economic climate the primary task of the workshop was to develop inexpensive furniture for manufacture by automated methods. Arndt and his students worked out standardised parts and studied methods of mass-production, moving away from a reliance on tubular steel to cheaper hybrids of wood and metal or pure wood designs.

Bauhaus furniture was described by Marcel Breuer as 'nothing but a necessary apparatus for contemporary life'. Its freely curving forms and daring structural arrangements belong to the machine aesthetic which the school helped to promote.

1   GROPIUS Armchair in cherrywood with yellow upholstery, 1923.
2   BREUER Easy chair, cherrywood with leather upholstery, c.1923. A modern version of the conventional easy chair, inspired by the aesthetics of Constructivism.
3   GROPIUS Director's office in the Weimar Bauhaus, 1923. The furniture was designed by Gropius and executed, together with the rugs, by students in the Bauhaus workshops.

3

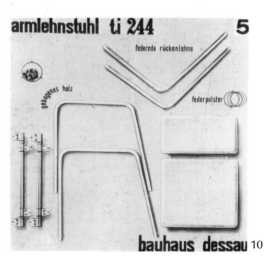

9   CABINETMAKING WORKSHOP Wood armchair with upholstered seat and back, c.1924.
10   ALBERS Armchair (ti 244) disassembled.
11   Bauhaus canteen, Dessau 1925, with stools designed and executed by Marcel Breuer in the cabinetmaking workshop. The stools, in nickel-plated tubular steel with painted wooden seats, were later manufactured commercially by Standard-Möbel.
12   Bauhaus auditorium, Dessau 1925, with tubular steel chairs by Marcel Breuer.
13   *Every day we are getting better and better* — a film sequence published in the *Bauhaus Journal* in 1926 showing Breuer's designs of 1921 (top two), 1922 (third) 1924 (fourth) and the original design for the 'Wassily' chair in tubular steel and canvas, 1925 (fifth). 'In the end we shall sit on resilient air columns', reads the caption for the sixth illustration.

4   ALBERS Armchair (ti 244), 1929, bentwood frame with tubular steel crossbar and spring upholstery.
5   CABINETMAKING WORKSHOP Folding deckchair (ti 240), 1929, wood frame with fabric seat and back.
6   CABINETMAKING WORKSHOP (attrib. Paul Reindel) Folding chair, 1930, in tubular steel and plywood.
7   BREDENDIECK Tubular steel and plywood chair, 1930.
8   DIECKMANN Wood chair with woven cane seat, after 1925. Although this chair was designed after Dieckmann had moved to the Weimar Staatliche Hochschule für Handwerk und Baukunst, it shows the influence of Breuer's ideas.

11
12

13

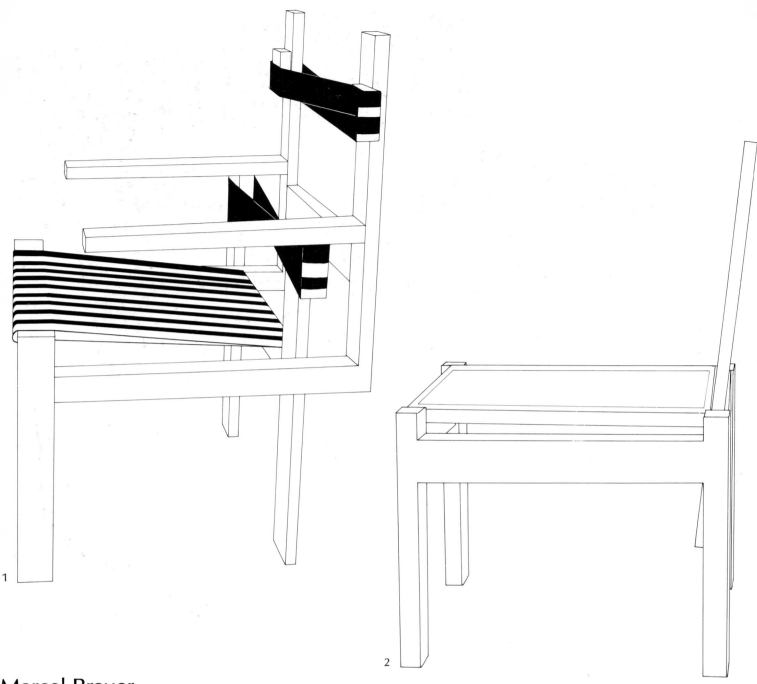

1

2

Marcel Breuer

b. 1902

Marcel Breuer left his native Hungary in 1920 to study painting at the Vienna Academy. Later in the same year he enrolled as a student at the Bauhaus, and by 1924 he was in charge of the furniture workshop. Breuer's preoccupation with standardised, modular unit furniture led him to an interest in standardised modular unit housing. In 1928 he set up an architectural practice in Berlin, designing flats in the Dolderthal district of Zürich (1933) with Alfred and Emil Roth which became one of the best known examples of the International Style in architecture. From 1935 to 1937 Breuer shared an architectural practice in London with F.R.S. Yorke and from 1937 to 1941 collaborated with Walter Gropius in the United States, during

which time he also taught architecture at Harvard University. He left Harvard in 1946 to set up a practice in New York, and recent commissions include the Unesco building, Paris (1952-58) with P. L. Nervi and B. Zehrfuss, and the Whitney Museum of American Art, New York (1966). He is also associated with the IBM design programme and has designed IBM laboratories at La Gaude, France and Boca Praton, Florida.

Marcel Breuer was one of the great pioneers of tubular steel chair design, and as early as 1925 he had invented a series of systems employing continuously bent steel tubes to form the structural frames of stools, chairs and tables. His 'Wassily' chair of the same year, which is still in production today, was the first chair in tubular

steel, and has become a classic of modern design.

Although Breuer's early student work, and even the 'Wassily' chair with its daring spatial arrangement, show the influence of the aesthetics of De Stijl and Constructivism, his interest soon shifted to a more practical concern with standardisation and economical mass-production. In the furniture he designed for the new Bauhaus premises in Dessau (1925) Breuer was given an unparalleled opportunity to test his ideas on a large scale, and the tubular steel chairs and stools for the auditorium and canteen were to provide the prototypes for many subsequent designs. By 1928 Breuer could claim in an advertisement for Standard-Möbel, the manufacturers of his furniture,

3

that 'one *type* [of chair] has been worked out for each of the required kinds of uses and improved to the point where no other variation is possible', and his cantilever chair of the same year is among the most commonly used modern commercial chairs in the world today.

Breuer continued his pioneering work in furniture design in the 1930s, developing for the English firm Isokon some of the first moulded plywood chairs to be manufactured in quantity, as well as some of the first chairs using an aluminium structural supporting frame. His designs are characterised by a functionalist concern to express each element separately, both in form and in material.

1   Armchair, 1922, wood with woven seat and backrest. A variation of this chair, designed originally as a student project, was used in the living room of the Bauhaus summer exhibition of 1923.
2   Wood chair with stretched fabric seat and back, 1924.
3, 4 'Wassily' chair, 1925, chromium nickel-plated tubular steel frame with leather seat, back and arms. The original version of the 'Wassily', used in Wassily Kandinsky's house on the Bauhaus campus at Dessau, was in tubular steel and canvas, with a straight back ending at the top of the canvas strap (see illustration 13, p. 121). The 'Wassily' was originally manufactured by Standard-Möbel, who also produced a folding version, and has formed part of the range of Gavina, Milan since 1965.

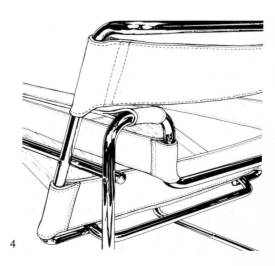

4

5

5   Cantilever chair ('Cesca'), 1928, chrome-plated tubular steel with seat and back of canework on an enamelled bentwood frame. This chair, the first of Breuer's cantilever designs, has been manufactured since 1965 by Gavina, and is now one of the most popular modern chairs.

6   Tubular steel dining chair, 1926, designed for Laszlo Moholy-Nagy's room at the Bauhaus in Dessau.

7   Folding chair, 1928, tubular steel with canvas seat and back.

8   Reclining armchair, 1928, tubular steel with cane seat and back. Exhibited at the Paris Werkbund exhibition of 1930.

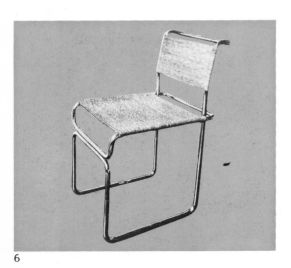

6

7

8

9

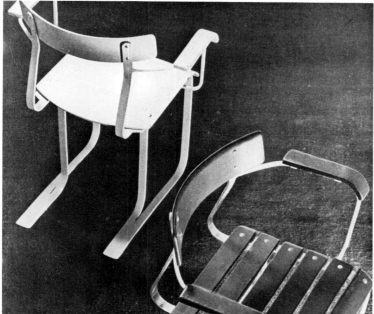

10

11

9   'Cesca' chair, 1928, model B with arms.
10   Aluminium chairs, 1933. Awarded first prize in the International Aluminium Competition, Paris 1933.
11   Chaise longue, 1935, bent beech

laminated frame with plywood seat. An upholstered version was manufactured from 1935 by Isokon, and from 1965 by Gavina.
12   Side chair in aluminium with padded leather seat and back, 1942.

13   Wooden nesting chairs, 1945.
14   Plywood chair with cane seat and back, designed for the 'International Competition for Low-Cost Furniture Design' organised by the Museum of Modern Art, New York in 1948.

12

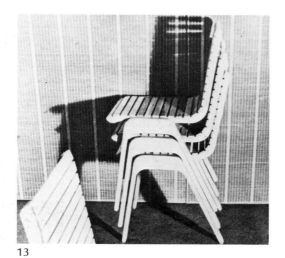

13

14

1

2

3

1   Cantilever tubular steel desk chair with
strap webbing, 1926. Manufactured from 1927
by L. & C. Arnold.
2   S34, chromium nickel-plated tubular steel
and leather. Manufactured from 1926 by
Thonet.
3   S33, chromium nickel-plated tubular steel
frame with canvas and later leather seat and
back, 1926. Originally executed by L. & C.
Arnold of Schorndorf, the S33 was later
manufactured by Thonet.

Mart Stam

b. 1899

The Dutch architect and designer Mart Stam trained at the Rijksnormaalschool voor Tekenonderwijs in Amsterdam, and then spent the years between 1919 and 1925 working in a succession of architectural practices in Amsterdam, Rotterdam, Berlin, Zürich and Thun. From 1925 until 1928 he was a member of the Opbouw group of architects in Holland, and he also collaborated with Emil Roth and Hans Schmidt in the publication of the architectural magazine *ABC* in Zürich.

Stam's architectural interest was in town-planning and housing rather than individual masterpieces, and he worked in this field in Russia from 1930 to 1934, in Rotterdam from 1941 and on the rebuilding of Dresden in 1949. He was a guest lecturer at the Bauhaus in 1928, and director of the Amsterdam Institute of Applied Art from 1939 until 1948, of the Dresden Akademie der Bildenden Künste from 1948 to 1950 and of the Kunstakademie Berlin-Weissensee from 1950 to 1953.

Stam's reputation as a chair designer rests almost exclusively on one design — the S33 — which was the first tubular steel cantilever chair. The idea originated from a chair made for his wife from straight lengths of tube and gas-fitters' 'L' joints, which he described to his fellow collaborators in the Stuttgart Weissenhofsiedlung exhibition at a preliminary conference in November 1926. Excited by the interest which the idea aroused, both Stam and Mies van der Rohe went away and produced cantilever chair designs within weeks of each other, although it was Mies who managed to get the patent for the principle of the resilient cantilever structure. Stam believed that 'it would be wrong to design our chairs larger or heavier than they need be, or for reasons of display. All they do is meet our requirements, that is to say, they should be light and mobile'. The S33, with its economical use of materials and reductive simplicity, is both functional and elegant, and a perfect expression of these principles.

Opposite:
1, 2, 3   LE CORBUSIER chaise longue, 1928;
basculant, 1929; siège tournant 1929.
Reproductions by Cassina.

1

2

3

4

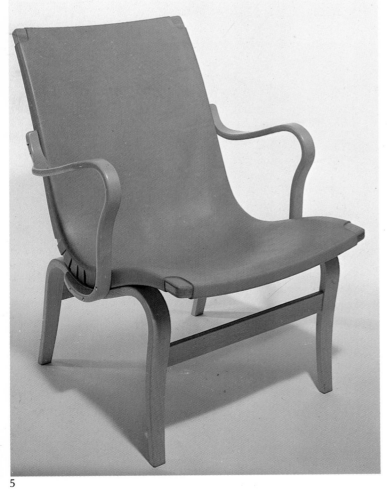

5

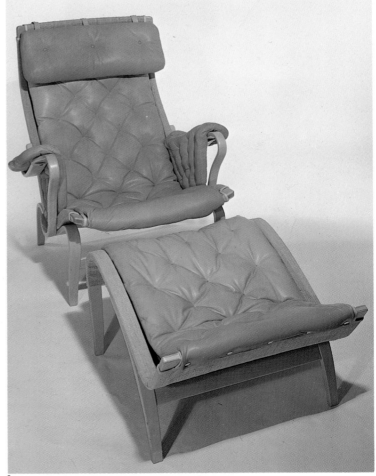

6

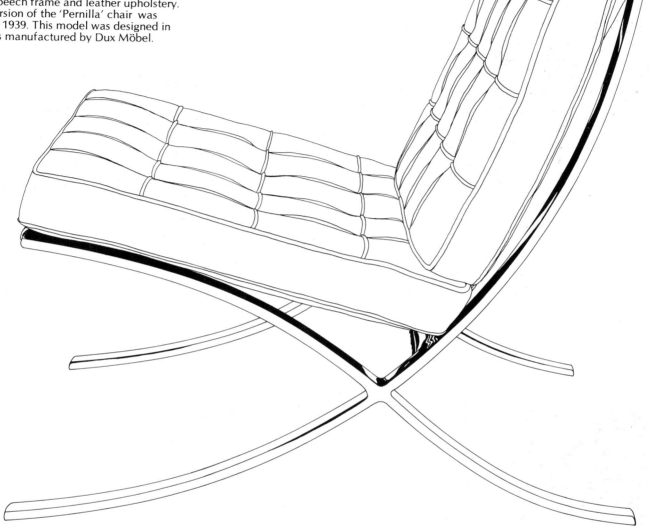

1

Ludwig Mies van der Rohe

1886-1969

Mies van der Rohe is generally recognised as one of the founding fathers of Modernism, and the most purist of Modern architects. His work is characterised by a constructional clarity, free-flowing space and careful detailing, in accordance with his famous maxim 'less is more'.

After two highly formative periods spent in the offices of Bruno Paul and Peter Behrens, Mies set up his own architectural practice in 1912. Although few of the projects of his early career were realised he extended his influence and reputation through his positions as director of the architectural section of the Novembergruppe (1921-25), vice-president of the Deutscher Werkbund (1926-32), organiser of the vast Weissenhofsiedlung housing

exhibition (1927) and director of the Bauhaus (1930-33). In 1938 he fled Nazi Germany to teach at the Illinois Institute of Technology in Chicago, and in 1948 he was made director. His work of the 1940s and 50s — various buildings at IIT, the Farnsworth house, Fox River (1946-50), Lake Shore Drive apartments, Chicago (1948-51) and the Seagram Office Building, New York (1954-58) — introduced the ideas of the European Modern Movement to America, and established his reputation as one of the most influential architects of the twentieth century.

Mies van der Rohe ranks as one of the most important twentieth-century chair designers, and the range of his designs — from the functional simplicity of the

cantilever chairs to the luxurious comfort of the Barcelona chair — is equalled only in the work of Charles Eames. Unlike Marcel Breuer or Mart Stam, he quickly discarded the constraints of functionalism and economical mass-production, with the result that his designs became works of art *per se*. Their careful detailing and feeling of space reflect the aesthetic concerns of his architecture.

Mies' first chair design was the MR, a cantilever tubular steel chair with leather seat and back, inspired by a prototype described by Mart Stam at a preliminary conference for the Weissenhofsiedlung housing exhibition in 1926. On August 24th 1927, Mies was granted the patent for the cantilever tubular steel chair, backed by his

2

3

4

claim to be 'the first to have exploited consistently the spring quality of steel tubes'. Several variations of the MR chair were produced, including a model with arms and models with canework seats and backs. His other designs using tubular steel include variations of a lounge chair and chaise longue with a continuous roll and pleat cushion and tubular steel frame (1931-32).

In 1929 Mies designed for his German pavilion at the Barcelona International Exhibition the famous Barcelona chair using a frame of chromium-plated steel strips, with horsehair cushions resting on leather straps. Mies intended the chairs to occupy specific places in his interiors, and indeed the weight of the frame ensures that the Barcelona chair is too heavy to be

easily moved. With the steel strip design and the 'X' joint, which had to be welded by hand in a laborious operation, all pretence of industrial production disappeared. The Barcelona chair has now become a classic example of luxurious design, and a status symbol of our time.

1   Barcelona chair, 1929, frame of flat steel bars, chrome-plated, in nine sections welded together; solid horsehair cushions with plain fabric or pigskin cover resting on seventeen

leather straps which are screwed into the frame. Although the chromed steel has now been replaced by stainless steel and the horsehair by foam rubber, the Barcelona chair is nevertheless almost entirely hand made. Originally manufactured by Joseph Müller and then Bamberg Metallwerkstätten of Berlin, it has been produced since 1948 by Knoll International.

2, 3, 4 Tugendhat chair, 1929-30, frame of flat steel bars, chrome-plated, in six sections (excluding arm pieces) connected by screws or welding, with two stiffening rods; solid horsehair cushions with plain fabric or pigskin cover resting on buckled leather straps which are wrapped around the frame. The original model, designed for the Tugendhat house, Brno, was executed by Joseph Müller of Berlin, and the chair has formed part of the range of Knoll International since 1964.

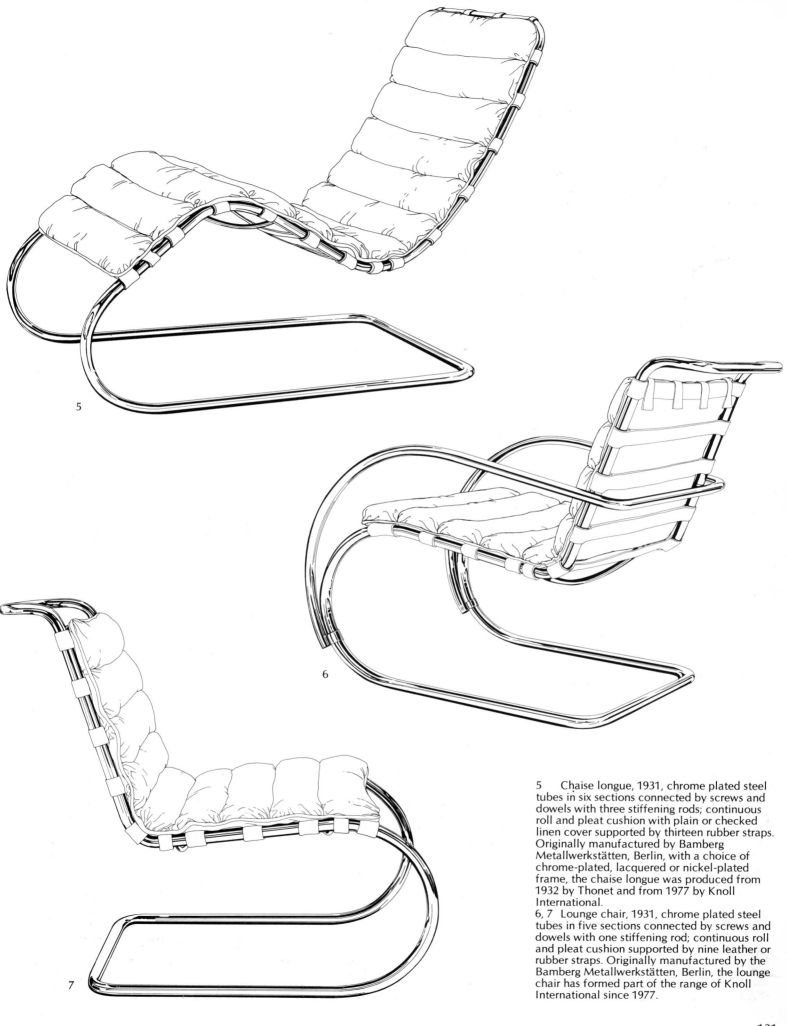

5   Chaise longue, 1931, chrome plated steel tubes in six sections connected by screws and dowels with three stiffening rods; continuous roll and pleat cushion with plain or checked linen cover supported by thirteen rubber straps. Originally manufactured by Bamberg Metallwerkstätten, Berlin, with a choice of chrome-plated, lacquered or nickel-plated frame, the chaise longue was produced from 1932 by Thonet and from 1977 by Knoll International.

6, 7   Lounge chair, 1931, chrome plated steel tubes in five sections connected by screws and dowels with one stiffening rod; continuous roll and pleat cushion supported by nine leather or rubber straps. Originally manufactured by the Bamberg Metallwerkstätten, Berlin, the lounge chair has formed part of the range of Knoll International since 1977.

9

10

11

8

12

8   Brno chair, 1929-30. Although the original model, designed for the Tugendhat house, Brno, used chromium-plated steel tubes and white calf upholstery, later versions have used flat steel bars in three sections which are screwed to the wooden seat and back. The Brno chair was originally manufactured by Joseph Müller and the Bamberg Metallwerkstätten of Berlin, and has been produced since 1977 by Knoll International.

9   MR chair with arms and lacquered cane seat, as used in the Tugendhat house, Brno in 1930.

10   MR chair, chrome-plated tubular steel in three sections connected by dowels and screws; leather seat and back attached with laces in this model, although the leather back of the original model was screwed to the frame. Originally designed for a room in the Weissenhofsiedlung housing exhibition, the MR chair was manufactured by Joseph Müller and

the Bamberg Metallwerkstätten, Berlin, and is currently produced by both Thonet and Knoll International.

11   Brno chair, current model.

12   Barcelona chair, current model.

13   German pavilion at the 1929 Barcelona exhibition, which formed the original setting for the Barcelona chair and ottoman. The pavilion was designed almost overnight, and its dimensions were determined by the onyx wall, made from the only available slab of onyx at the local retailers. Designed as a setting for the inaugural ceremony in which the Spanish King Alfonso XIII was to sign his name in a golden book, the pavilion contained two Barcelona chairs for the King and Queen with several ottomans set at a discreet distance.

14   Lounge chair with bed and bedside table by Lilly Reich, presented as part of a model house by Lilly Reich at the Berlin building exhibition of 1931.

13

14

1

Le Corbusier

1887-1965

Le Corbusier was the most influential and best-known architect of the twentieth century, and his radical proposals in the fields of town-planning, public building, housing and design represented a totally new approach to the problem of catering for modern life. Earlier than any other architect he realised that new methods of building required not only a functional approach, but a completely new aesthetic, and his theories and work have had a determining influence on the course of Modern architecture.

Le Corbusier was born in Switzerland as Charles-Edouard Jeanneret, and studied at the School of Applied Arts, La Chaux-de-Fonds. The major part of his education, however, was gained during the years 1907 to 1910, when he travelled in Europe sketching buildings and meeting many of the most important architects of the period — Josef Hoffmann, in whose office he worked for some months; the pioneer of reinforced concrete Auguste Perret; and Peter Behrens, who introduced him to modern design through his own work and his contact with the Deutscher Werkbund.

During the next twelve years Le Corbusier defined his ideas through a series of projects and writings — the Domino houses (1914), the Citrohan houses (1920-21) and his articles on architecture for the periodical *L'Esprit Nouveau,* which he founded in 1920 in collaboration with Amédée Ozenfant. His belief in houses as 'machines for living in', using basic geo-

2

3

metrical shapes with a total rejection of all applied ornament, found its concrete expression in buildings such as the Pavillon de l'Esprit Nouveau at the Paris 1925 exhibition, the Villa Stein, Garches (1927) and the Villa Savoye at Poissy (1929-30).

During the 1930s Le Corbusier worked on revolutionary town-planning schemes and large-scale projects such as the Pavillon Suisse for the University of Paris, which subsequently became the model for hundreds of halls of residence, and for his own Unités d'Habitation in Marseille (1947-52). He continued to work until his death, and his major projects include the Chapel of Ronchamp (1950), the monastery of La Tourette (1954-59) and a scheme for Chandigarh (1950-70).

Le Corbusier's furniture, like his architecture, was based on the realisation that new methods of production, materials and social trends necessitated a new approach to the problems of design. His willingness to totally rethink existing conventions resulted in forms which were both functional and aesthetically pleasing, and his chairs are now recognised as landmarks in the history of design.

Le Corbusier used Thonet chairs in his early houses, and his own chairs show a similar concern to produce an anonymous product suitable for mass-production. His basic designs — the grand confort and chaise longue (1928), the basculant and siège tournant (1929) and the canapé (1935) — were produced in several variations, and

4

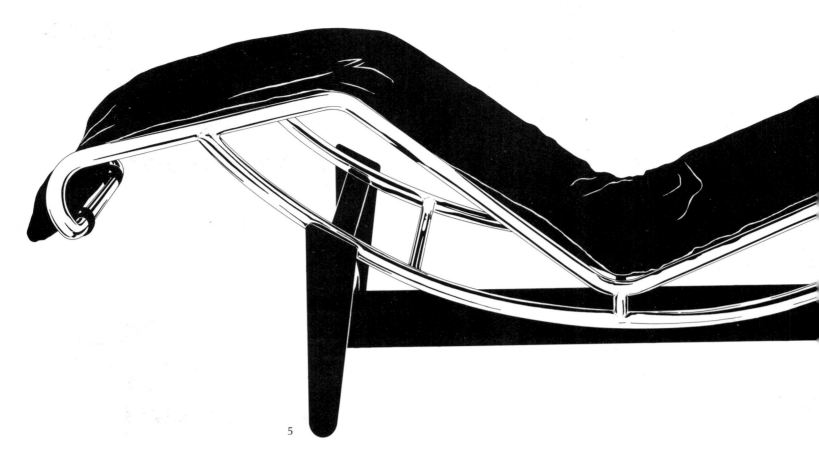

5

8

9

are characterised by their clean, geometrical lines and exposed structural
elements. Comfort was ensured by
allowing the occupant a choice of position,
either through their size or a built-in
flexibility, and their validity as standard
units, based on typical proportions and
designed to fulfill typical needs and
functions, is proved by the fact that they
are still in widespread demand today.

The designs attributed to Le Corbusier
were produced during a period of collaboration with his cousin Pierre Jeanneret
and Charlotte Perriand. They were
originally manufactured by Thonet, and
have been mass-produced since the late
1950s by H. Weber in Germany, and more
recently by Cassina in Italy.

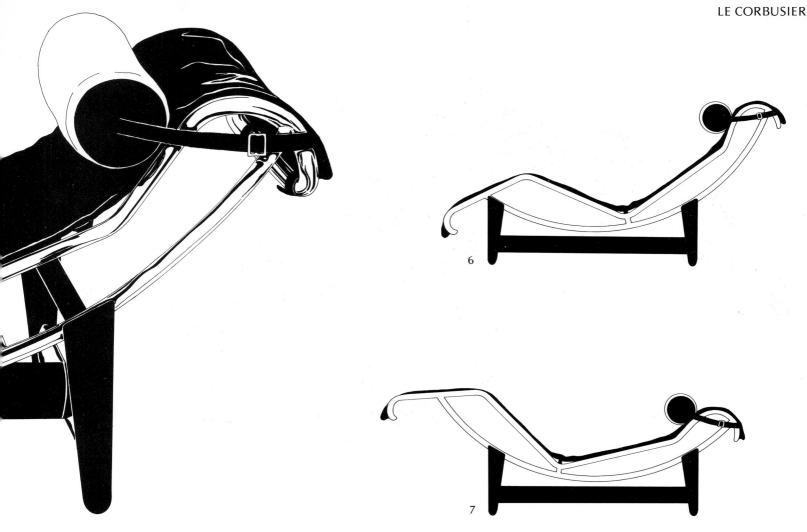

1, 2 Basculant, 1929, polished or chrome-plated steel tube frame, black leather armrests, ponyskin or leather seat and back. The basculant, with its basic cubic form, strap arms and mobile back, which is fixed on two points and moves by turning on its axis, was inspired by the 'Safari' chair, used by Le Corbusier in his early interiors. Originally manufactured by Thonet, and more recently by Cassina, it is the most complex of Le Corbusier's designs.

3, 4 Grand confort, 1928, chrome-plated or polished steel tube frame on which are placed cushions to form seat, back and sides. Originally manufactured by Thonet, and more recently by Cassina.

5, 6, 7 Chaise longue, 1928, polished or chrome-plated steel tube frame with fabric or ponyskin cover, iron base. The chaise longue was the first to be made adjustable by simply moving the whole frame, which rests freely on the iron trestle. Le Corbusier was working on a version of a chaise longue as early as 1922 for his immeuble-villas, and variations using laminated wood were designed for Thonet in 1932. This model was originally manufactured by Thonet, and has been produced since 1965 by Cassina.

8   Interior of a house at the Stuttgart Weissenhofsiedlung exhibition, 1927-28, with basculant and chaise longue.

9   Dining room designed by Charlotte Perriand for the Salon des Artistes Décorateurs, 1928, with sièges tournants in tubular steel with padded red leather seats and backs, and swivel stools in tubular steel with green leather cushions.

10   'Equipement intérieur d'une habitation', designed by Le Corbusier, Perriand and Pierre Jeanneret for the 1929 Salon d'Automne, and including the basculant, siège tournant, chaise longue and grand confort.

1

2

3

4

PEL
Practical Equipment Ltd

Practical Equipment Limited was formed in July 1931 by Tube Investments, a company founded in 1919 from a merger of Accles and Pollock, Tubes Limited and several smaller companies to avoid a return to the cut-throat rivalry which had existed in the Midlands steel tube industry before the war. Early in 1931 two directors from Tube Investments, Captain P. G. Carew and Major Higgins, had noticed two tubular steel chairs in the foyer of the Strand Palace Hotel. Realising the immense potential of furniture as an outlet for steel tube, Carew persuaded Tube Investments to form a new company with himself as managing director and Oliver Bernard as design consultant.

From the beginning Pel aimed for an affluent, fashionable clientele, and the Prince of Wales, Mrs Simpson and the Indian royalty were among the visitors to their stylish showrooms in Henrietta Street, London. The influence of Oliver Bernard is very apparent in their early output, and his adventurous designs with their gracefully inflected curves were to influence production long after he had ceased to work directly for the firm. Pel was also able to rise above many of its rivals through the sheer quality of its seamless tubing, manufactured by the experienced Accles and Pollock.

Pel's first important commission was for the BBC's Broadcasting House (1928-30). The publicity the building received led to a flood of orders, and

6

7

through this commission Carew also met Wells Coates, Serge Chermayeff and Raymond McGrath, all of whom were subsequently to produce designs for the company. In April 1932 Pel had a stand at the Ideal Home Exhibition which led to orders from Claridges, the Savoy Hotel and Harrods. As the decade progressed, however, increased production and lower prices meant that the furniture became less exclusive, and the firm concentrated on functional standardisation and efficiency rather than adventurous design for its own sake. Pel is still in existence today, and its stacking chairs such as the RP6 have become a standard feature in schools, church halls and public buildings throughout the world.

1   RP6 nesting chair, chromed or enamelled tubular steel frame, canvas seat and back.
2   'Nesting armchair', chromed or enamelled tubular steel frame, canvas or upholstered seat and back, 1931-32. The nesting armchair was a prototype for the RP7, a version with arms of the RP6.
3   SP9, 1932-34. Like the other Pel designs for armchairs and office chairs, the SP9 was available in chromed or enamelled tubular steel frame with calico, rexine or hide upholstery.
4   SP4, 1931-32.
5   RP6, SP3 (Pel's adaptation of Mart Stam's S33), RP7 and SP4B (a fully upholstered version of the SP4), side elevations.
6   RP10 swivelling office armchair, 1933-36.
7   SP7, 1932-33.
8   A variation of the SP11 with cut-away sides 1932-36.

8

1

Alvar Aalto

1898-1976

Alvar Aalto was one of the most important Scandinavian architects and designers of the twentieth century, and is largely responsible for his native Finland's high reputation in the fields of architecture and furniture design. A recognised master of the Modern Movement, Aalto was nevertheless unique among his contemporaries in the emphasis he placed on warmth, naturalness and respect for human feelings — a contrast to the often rigid functionalism and didacticism of mainstream Modernism.

After studying architecture at the University of Helsinki, Aalto spent some time in architectural offices in Sweden before setting up his own practice in Turku in 1927. In the course of his career he com-

pleted over two hundred buildings and projects including major commissions for civic centres, libraries and university buildings. Characteristically his work combines a careful study of the technical principles of such areas as lighting, heating, acoustics and solar orientation with an understanding of natural site qualities and an imaginative handling of form and materials.

Aalto saw furniture as 'accessories to architecture', and described his aim as the creation of 'multi-dimensional, sculpture-like wooden forms... organic volumes made of wood without resorting to cutting or carving'. His first modern chair design was for his Jyväskylä Civil Guard building of 1927, for which he produced a stacking

chair with straight legs and supports and a plywood seat and back. In 1929, as a result of his belief that the human body should come into contact only with organic materials, he began experimenting with new methods of bending wood and effective glues developed in the aero-industry at the workshop of a local furniture manufacturer Otto Korhonen. The first result of a long association with design experimentation was a moulded plywood stacking chair supported on bent metal pipes, replaced in later models by laminated wood, which was exhibited in Korhonen's installation at the seventh centenary exhibition in Turku in 1929.

Between 1930 and 1933 Aalto developed the 'Paimio' chair made of birch

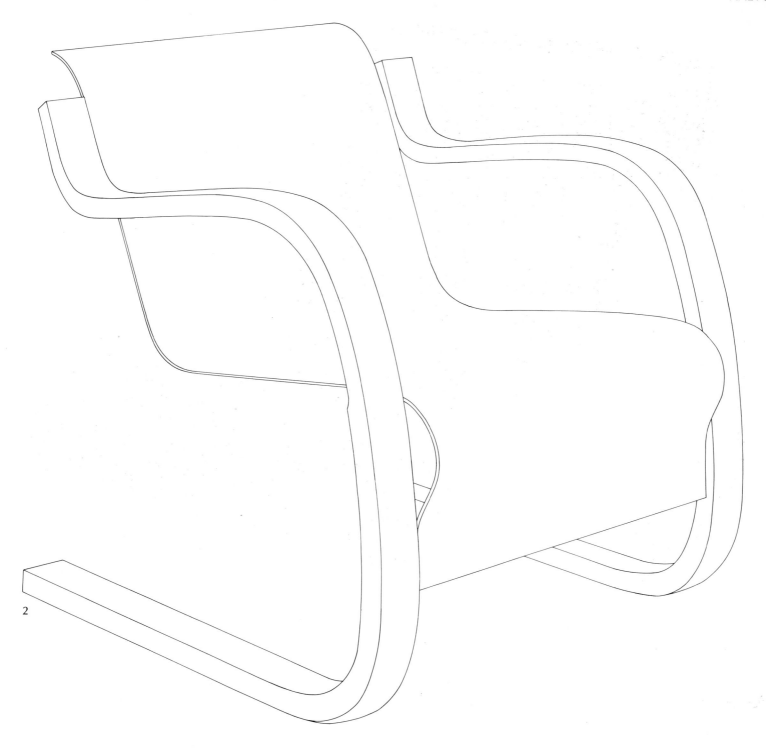

2

veneer layers, and experimented with methods of forming a bent structural support of laminated wood, perfected in his stools for the Viipuri library (1933). Designers had been trying to produce an all plywood chair since 1876, and in 1935 Aalto finally succeeded with his spring-leaf chair, which depended on a compression spring of birch veneers welded together. The spring-leaf chair was produced in a variety of shapes and profiles including an upholstered version, and a chaise longue and easy chair were later developed using the same principle.

Like his architecture Aalto's chair designs represent a 'humanised' interpretation of the severe aesthetic and radical technological experimentation of the Modern Movement, as exemplified by the spring-leaf chair which is a softer, more organic version in wood of the tubular steel cantilever designs of Marcel Breuer and Mart Stam. His furniture is still in production today, and is manufactured by Artek, the firm founded in the early 1930s by Aalto himself, his first wife and Maire Gullichsen as 'a centre for contemporary furniture, home furnishings, art and industrial art'.

1, 3 'Paimio' chair, 1930-33, seat and back of plywood moulded on two different forms, continuous arms and legs of birch veneer layers.
2 Spring-leaf chair, moulded plywood seat supported on a compression spring of seven birch veneers, 1935.

3

4   Armchair 406, 1935-39. A variation of the spring-leaf chair with seat of canvas webbing on a spring-leaf frame. Canvas or hemp webbing seats became a feature of Scandinavian design, and were used in particular by Bruno Mathsson.
5   Stool, 1954.
6, 7 Stacking stools for the discussion and lecture hall of the Viipuri library, 1929-33. A flexibility and springiness were obtained by cutting the solid wood of the legs, which are attached by screws to the wooden seats, laterally at the point of bending.
Opposite
Stool and table, 1954. The perfect integration of the bent, solid wood legs with the seat of the stool and the table top make this design the nearest to Aalto's ideal of 'multi-dimensional sculpture-like wooden forms'.

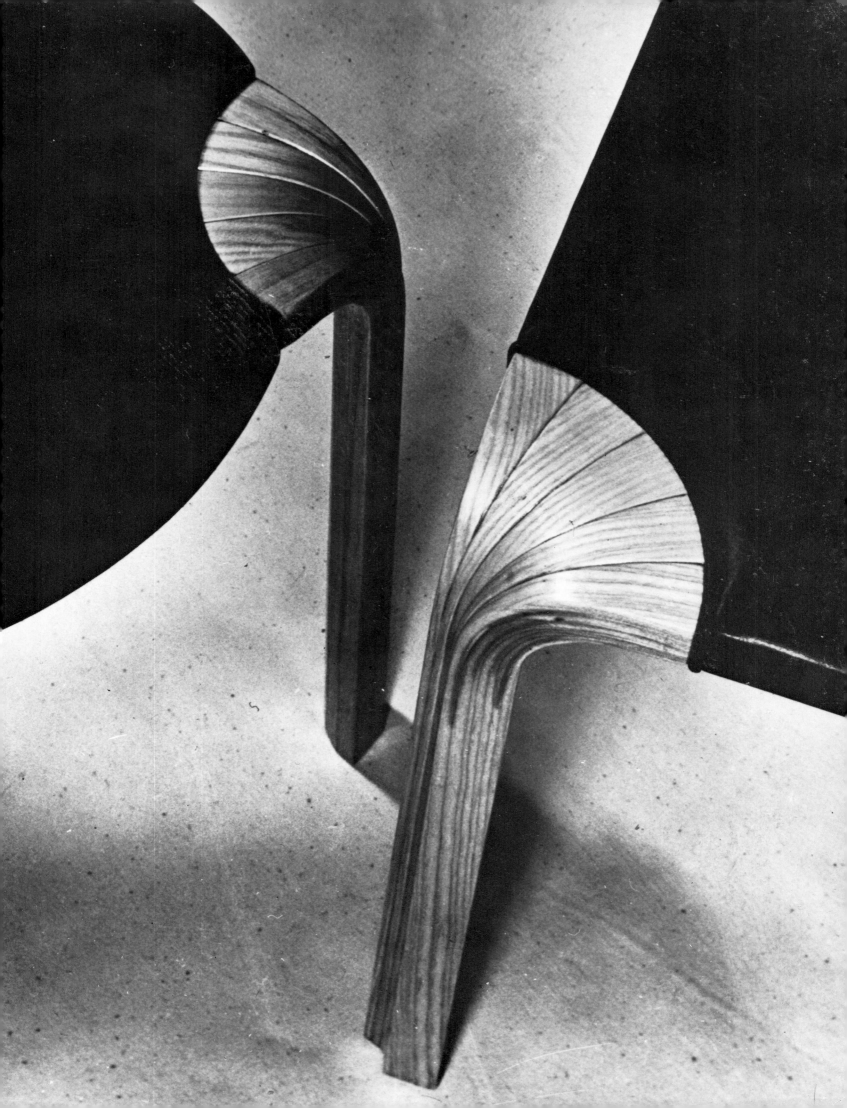

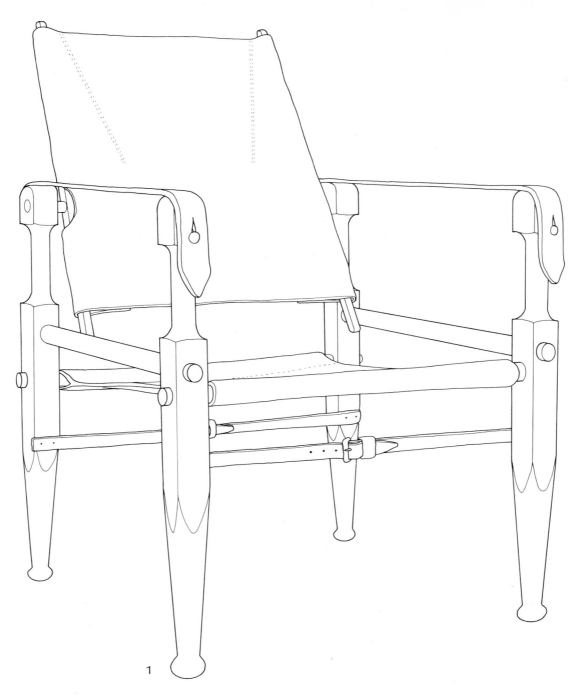

1

Kaare Klint

1888-1954

Kaare Klint trained as a painter before working as an architect in the offices of his father, P. V. Jensen Klint, and Carl Peterson with whom he collaborated from 1912 to 1915. In 1920 he opened his own practice in Copenhagen, and he worked as a professor of architecture from 1944.

Klint's major interest, however, was in furniture, and from 1924 through his position as director of the School of Cabinet-Making at the Copenhagen Academy of Arts he trained a generation of designers and laid the foundations of modern Danish furniture design. Klint's goal was to create timeless, eminently practical furniture — what he called 'tools for living' — with fitness for purpose as its major criterion. He conducted systematic

studies into the theoretical principles, physiological correctness and function of furniture, and attempted to adapt a number of time-tested, earlier forms to the functional and aesthetic needs of the present. His chair designs are often based on anonymous traditional models, and are characterised by a practical simplicity. They were manufactured by N. M. Rasmussen, N. C. Jensen Kjaer and Rud. Rasmussen of Copenhagen, who maintain the production of his designs today.

1   'Safari' chair, 1933, solid wood frame with slung canvas or leather seat and back.
2   Deck chair, 1933, collapsible teak frame with cane seat and back panels. The foot-rest extends to form a chaise longue.

2

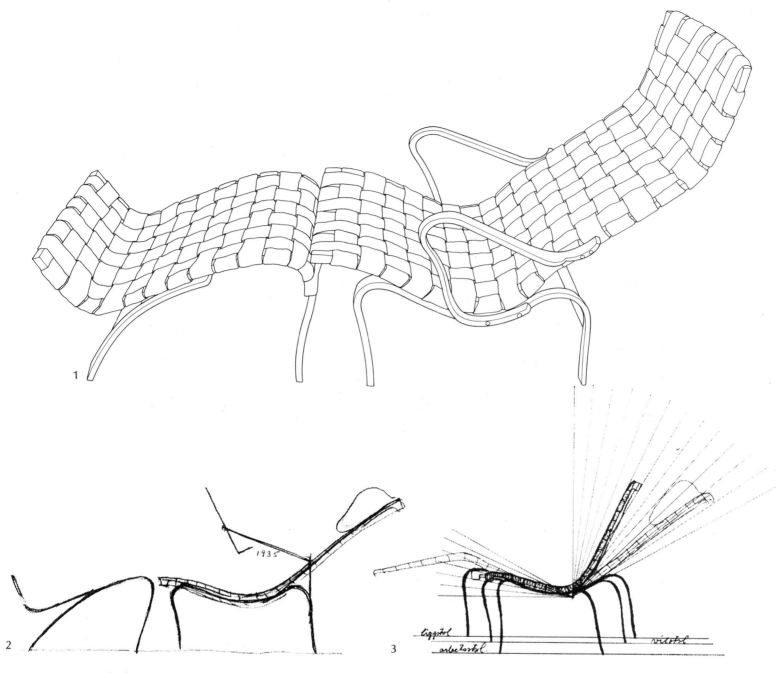

Bruno Mathsson

b. 1907

The Swedish architect and designer Bruno Mathsson trained in the office of his father, Karl Mathsson, a master cabinet-maker who executed many of his son's early designs. His work has been exhibited throughout Europe and America, and he was awarded the Gregor-Paulsson trophy in 1955.

Mathsson's chair designs are based on his own detailed anatomical studies of the sitting posture, and his investigations into the relationship between chair seat, backrest and floor. The most important period of his career were the years 1933 to 1935, when he used his findings to develop a range of chairs which were to form the basis of his subsequent designs. His chairs of the 1930s have a seat made up of a moulded wood frame covered with tightly stretched webbing (a design also used by Alvar Aalto), which rests on flexible plywood legs. Like all his designs, seat and substructure are treated separately, and comfort is ensured through flexibility and elasticity.

1 Lounge chair and ottoman, 1935, lower frame of natural bent laminated wood with seat and back of hemp webbing on a solid wood frame. Manufactured by Karl Mathsson.
2 Lounge chair with headrest and reading plate, 1935.
3 Diagram showing the three basic forms of the Mathsson chair, developed between 1933 and 1935.
4 Own summer house, Frösakull, Holland 1961.

1

2

3

4

Hans Wegner

b. 1914

Hans Wegner trained at the Copenhagen School of Arts and Crafts before opening his own office in 1943. His work which includes designs for furniture, silverware, lamps and wallpapers, has received widespread acclaim, and was awarded medals at the Milan Triennales, the Lunning Prize (1954) and the AID Award USA (1961). Wegner has worked as a design consultant to several Danish furniture manufacturers, and was a lecturer at the Copenhagen School of Arts and Crafts from 1946 to 1953.

Wegner's chair designs are a synthesis of precision construction, imagination and truth to his favoured material — wood. They are characterised by an extreme simplicity, with a lightness and spareness of form which makes them eminently suitable for mass-production. His chairs are manufactured by Salesco, a company formed from the amalgamation of five separate factories and devoted exclusively to producing his designs.

1   'The chair', 1949, teak with woven cane or upholstered seat.
2   Chair 24, 1950, oak or beech with a choice of nine lacquer finishes, paper-cord seat, and armrest bent under steam pressure.
3   Folding chair, 1949, teak with woven cane seat and back.
4   Vacation house with a version of the chair 24 in lacquered oak.
Opposite
Wood chair with paper-cord seat, inspired by a traditional model and manufactured by Johannes Hansen.

1

2

The Festival of Britain

1951

The Festival of Britain Exhibition, commemorating by its date the Great Exhibition of 1851, was intended as a demonstration of an optimistic Britain bursting with new talent and new design ideas after the grey war years. It was housed in a complex of specially designed buildings on London's South Bank including the Royal Festival Hall, and the interior design section was based around the themes of the bed-sitting room, the kitchen, hobbies in the home, entertainment at home and the parlour. A presentation panel, headed by the general organiser Gerald Barry, selected certain interior designers for each theme who were given a free hand to design stands and furnish them with existing pieces chosen from a stock list compiled by

the Council of Industrial Design. As well as the furnishing of the stands, however, the exhibition also provided opportunities for designers in the furnishing of the numerous cafés, restaurants and entertainment halls provided for the public.

The Festival of Britain brought to the public's attention a new generation of designers — notably Robin Day, Clive Latimer, Ernest Race, Howard Keith, Dennis Young and Lucian Ercolani — and helped to crystallise post-war trends into a distinctive style. The chair designs depended strongly on the exploitation of new materials — new alloys, synthetic upholstery and mouldable materials. Their most notable characteristics include an emphasis on lightness, with seat and sub-

structure almost invariably treated separately; slender, tapering legs; and a widespread use of bright colours.

1, 2 RACE Dining or office chair, 1945, cast aluminium frame with padded plywood seat and back, with or without arms and with vinyl, hide or fabric upholstery. Designed to use resmelted aluminium alloy from wartime scrap, these chairs were first shown at the 'Britain Can Make It' exhibition of 1946, and won a gold medal at the 10th Milan Triennale in 1951. Over 250,000 were manufactured by Race Furniture Ltd, Sheerness.

4

5

6

3

3   YOUNG Shell chair, jute-reinforced 'Fibrenyle' thermo-plastic shell, legs and frame of steel rod, seat cushion and head support of latex foam with 'Somic' pile fabric upholstery.
4   Café in the Homes and Gardens Pavilion designed by Bronek Katz and R. Vaughan, with 'antelope' chairs by Ernest Race in painted white metal with wood seats.
5   Thameside Restaurant, with metal and wood chairs designed by Neville Ward and Frank Austin.
6   Homes and Gardens Pavilion, 'entertainment at home', by Robin Day. A music lover's room, with upholstered easy chairs with metal frames.
7   Homes and Gardens Pavilion, divan-settee in solid bent ash with Latex foam cushions submitted in the 'bed-sitting room' section by C. F. Matthew. The back pivots to form a divan.

7

The Milan School

Milan's position as one of Italy's major creative and industrial centres arose after the First World War due to a liberal co-operation between big business, small workshops and progressive designers. During the 1930s the pioneering work of architects such as Giuseppe Terragni and the Novecento group, who set out to restore plastic values and a sense of volume in architecture in opposition to the rigour of the International Style, transformed the whole spectrum of industrial design. The additional international stimulation of the Milan Triennale, inaugurated in 1923, and the pioneering approach of magazines such as *Domus* and *Casabella* combined to put Italy in the forefront of furniture design. After the Second World War archi-

tects concentrated on rebuilding residential areas and raising the standards of economically produced apartments and furniture, and as an incentive the department store La Rinascente introduced a prize for functional, modern furniture awarded at the Triennale.

Important designers of the Milan School include Osvaldo Borsani, Franco Albini, Carlo de Carli, Renzo Zavanella and Carlo Enrico Rava. Especially innovative is the work of Carlo Mollino, whose playful, sculptural chair designs, manufactured by Appelli and Varesio and Cellerino, constitute a distinctive and imaginative version of organic modernism.

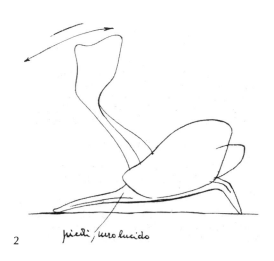

3

1, 2   MOLLINO Fully upholstered reclining easy chair, 1949, together with Mollino's preliminary sketch. The easy chair was manufactured by the Torinese firm Cellerino.
3   RAVA Side chair with upholstered seat, 1948.
4   TERRAGNI Chair in steel and wood, c.1935-36.
5   ALBINI Rocking chair in iron, 1940.
6   PONTI Black stained wood chair with wicker set, 1952.
7   ALBINI, COLOMBINI and SGRELLI Armchair with adjustable seat and back, wood frame with foam rubber upholstery, c.1950. Manufactured by La Rinascente.

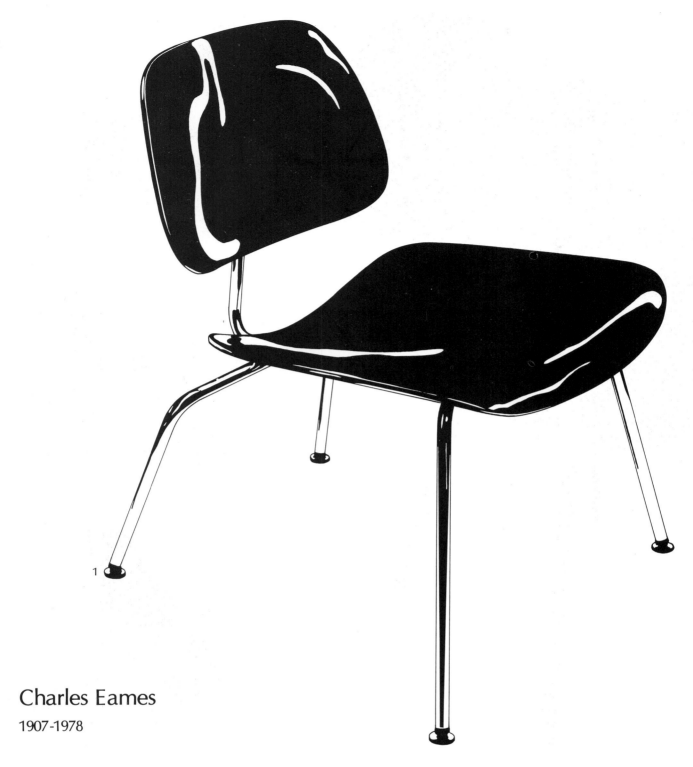

1

Charles Eames

1907-1978

The American architect and designer Charles Eames studied architecture at Washington University, St. Louis and in 1930 set up his own office. In 1936 he accepted a fellowship at Cranbrook Academy of Art, where he met his future collaborator Eero Saarinen, son of the director Eliel Saarinen, and a year later he was made head of the Department of Experimental Design. Eames moved with his wife to Southern California in 1941, continuing his experiments in furniture design and building two adjacent houses for himself and John Entenza in 1949 which were hailed as radical demonstrations of prefabrication. Eames was one of the architects selected by Eliot Noyes to contribute to IBM's new corporate design pro-

gramme, and was a regular contributor to the annual IDCA conferences in Colorado.

Charles Eames was undoubtedly one of the most influential designers of the twentieth century. His first major success came in 1940 when, in collaboration with Eero Saarinen, he produced the winning chair designs for the Museum of Modern Art's competition 'Organic Design in Home Furnishings'. Exhibited at the Museum in 1941, these chairs were innovative in their use of plywood shells moulded not in one direction as in the work of Aalto or Breuer, but in two directions to create a truly 'sculptural', three-dimensional effect. Production was held up because the cycle-welding process of joining wood to metal developed by the Chrysler Corporation was

reserved for military purposes during the war, and the chairs were finally manufactured by Herman Miller Inc. using wooden legs.

From 1941, Eames and his wife experimented with low-cost techniques for wood lamination and moulding and in 1946, at a one-man show at the Museum of Modern Art, a new set of moulded plywood chairs were exhibited including the seminal 'Eames chair'. This side chair of moulded plywood with metal rod legs was made in several variations including one entirely in wood, although Eames preferred to treat seat and substructure as two quite separate components. Also included in the exhibition was an innovative design for a chair with a projecting rear leg shorter than the

3

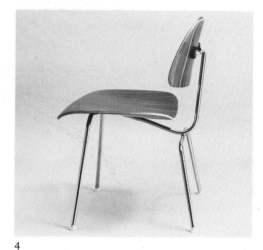

4

2

5

others to enable the sitter to recline by tilting the chair back. Eames won second prize in the 'International Competition for Low-Cost Furniture Design' of 1948 with a series of chairs including a one-piece shell-like chaise longue intended to be manufactured in stamped aluminium but eventually produced in moulded polyester. He continued to design for the rest of his life, producing influential pieces such as the 'aluminium group' of 1958, made of polished aluminium padded with vinyl foam, and the swivel lounge chair and ottoman (1956) from moulded rosewood shells with black leather cushions and a polished aluminium base.

Eames considered himself primarily an architect, stating that he could not help

'but look at the problems around us as problems of structure — and structure is architecture'. He seldom worked from drawings, preferring to work out his designs at full scale to allow frequent tests for comfort. Many of his chairs were never manufactured, but used as a basis for more successful designs.

1 'Eames chair', 1946, moulded walnut plywood seat and back, stained black, with chrome-plated steel rod frame and rubber shock mounts.
2 DAR chair, 1950, shell seat in moulded polyester reinforced with glass fibres, chromium-plated steel legs attached to the shell by means of the rubber shock mounts used on the 'Eames chair'. Eames' DAR chairs

represented the first use of glass fibre in seating, and were manufactured by Herman Miller Inc. in several permutations made up from Eames' interchangeable designs for shells and supports. The range developed from Eames' submission to the Museum of Modern Art's 'International Competition for Low-Cost Furniture Design' of 1948.
3 Dining chair, 1946, in moulded and bent birch plywood.
4 Dining chair, 1946, moulded walnut or ash plywood seat and back, chrome-plated steel rod frame.
5 Side chair, 1955, shell seat in moulded polyester reinforced with glass fibres, zinc-coated steel tube legs and rubber shock mounts, manufactured by Herman Miller Inc. in a variety of colours. The hooks on the side of the legs are for stability when stacking the chair.

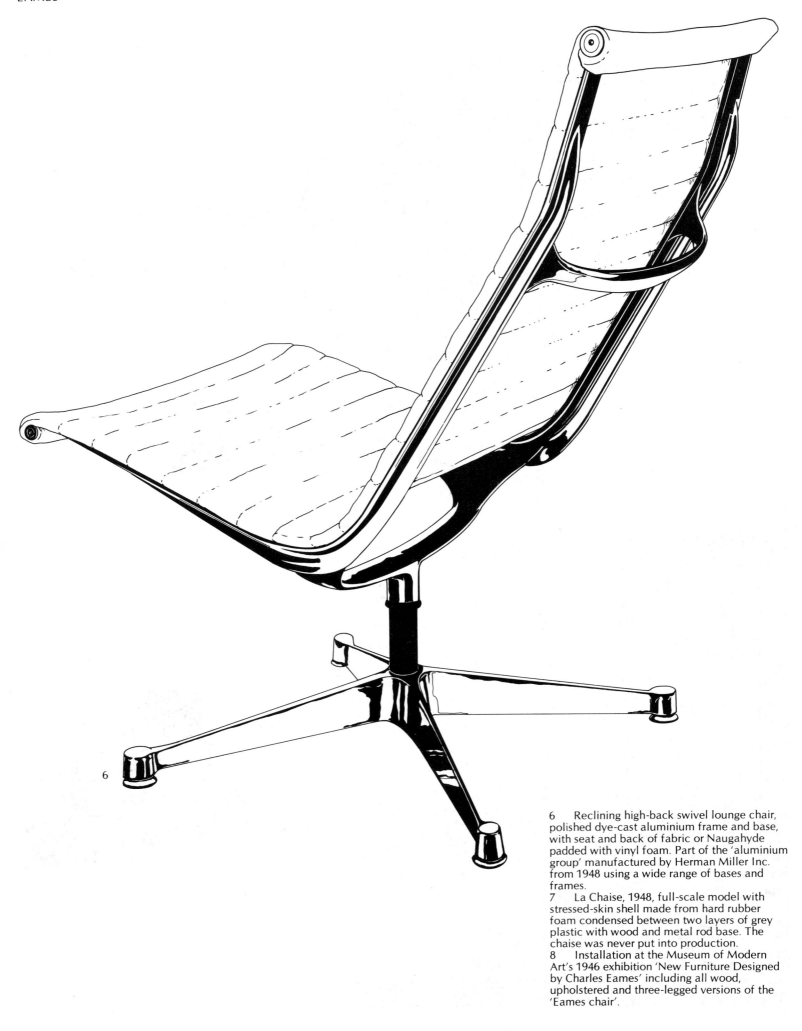

6

6   Reclining high-back swivel lounge chair, polished dye-cast aluminium frame and base, with seat and back of fabric or Naugahyde padded with vinyl foam. Part of the 'aluminium group' manufactured by Herman Miller Inc. from 1948 using a wide range of bases and frames.

7   La Chaise, 1948, full-scale model with stressed-skin shell made from hard rubber foam condensed between two layers of grey plastic with wood and metal rod base. The chaise was never put into production.

8   Installation at the Museum of Modern Art's 1946 exhibition 'New Furniture Designed by Charles Eames' including all wood, upholstered and three-legged versions of the 'Eames chair'.

7

8

Bibliography

Books

Agius, Pauline, *British Furniture 1880-1915*, Woodbridge 1978.
Alison, Filippo, *Charles Rennie Mackintosh as a Designer of Chairs*, London 1978.
Amaya, Mario, *Art Nouveau*, London 1971.
Andrews, Edward Deming and Faith, *Shaker Furniture: The Craftsmanship of an American Communal Sect*, New York 1937.
Anscombe, Isabelle, and Gere, Charlotte, *Arts and Crafts in Britain and America*, London 1978.
Argan, Giulio Carlo, *Marcel Breuer: disegno industriale e architettura*, Milan 1957.
Aslin, Elizabeth, *Nineteenth-Century English Furniture*, London 1962.
Bairiti, Eleonora, Bossaglia, Rossana, and Rosci, Mario, *L'Italia Liberty*, Milan 1973.
Bangert, Albrecht, *Thonet-Möbel*, Munich 1979.
Banham, Reyner, *Theory and Design in the First Machine Age*, London 1960.
Barilli, Renato, *Art Nouveau*, London 1969.
Baroni, Daniele, *Gerrit Thomas Rietveld Furniture*, London 1978.
Bestetti, Carlo, *Forme nuove in Italia*, Rome 1957.
Billcliffe, Roger, *Charles Rennie Mackintosh: The Complete Furniture, Furniture Drawings and Interior Designs*, Guildford and London 1979.
Bishop, Robert, *Centuries and Styles of the American Chair, 1640-1970*, New York 1972.
Blake, Peter, *Marcel Breuer: Architect and Designer*, New York 1949.
Blaser, Werner (ed.), *Folding Chairs*, Basle, Boston and Stuttgart 1982.
Blaser, Werner, *Mies van der Rohe: Möbel und Interieurs*, Stuttgart 1981.
Bossaglia, Rossana, *Art Nouveau: Revolution in Interior Design*, London 1973.
Brunhammer, Yvonne, *Le Style 1925*, Paris n.d.
Buffet-Challié, Laurence, *Le Moderne Style*, Paris n.d.
Campbell-Cole, Barbie, Benton, Tim, and Banham, Reyner, *Tubular Steel Furniture*, London 1979.
Candilis, George, et al., *Bugholzmöbel*, Stuttgart 1980.
Champigneulle, Bernard, *Art Nouveau*, London 1976.
Dal Fabbro, Mario, *Furniture for Modern Interiors*, New York 1954.
Dalisi, Riccardo, *Gaudí, mobili e oggetti*, Milan 1979.

De Fusco, Renato, *Le Corbusier, Designer: Furniture, 1929*, Milan and New York 1976.
Domergue, Denise, *Artists Design Furniture*, New York 1984.
Duncan, Alistair, *Art Deco Furniture*, London n.d.
Duncan, Alistair, *Art Nouveau Furniture*, London n.d.
Edwards, Ralph, *A History of the English Chair*, London 1951.
Emery, Marc, *Furniture by Architects: 500 International Masterpieces of 20th-Century Design and Where to Buy Them*, New York n.d.
Frey, Gilbert, *The Modern Chair: 1850 to Today*, Teufen 1970.
Garner, Philippe (ed.), *Phaidon Encyclopedia of Decorative Arts 1890-1940*, Oxford 1978.
Garner, Philippe, *Emile Gallé*, London 1976.
Greenberg, Cara, *Mid-Century Modern: Furniture of the 1950s*, London 1985.
Hanks, David A., *The Decorative Designs of Frank Lloyd Wright*, London 1979.
Hart, Harold, *Chairs Through the Ages: A Pictorial Archive of Woodcuts and Engravings*, New York 1977.
Haslam, Malcolm, Garner, Philippe, Harvey, Mary, and Conway, Hugh, *The Amazing Bugattis*, London 1979.
Hennessey, William J., *Modern Furnishings for the Home* (2 vols.), New York 1952.
Hiort, Esbjorn, *Modern Danish Furniture*, New York n.d.
Joel, David, *The Adventure of British Furniture 1851-1951*, London 1953.
Larner, Gerald and Celia, *The Glasgow Style*, Edinburgh 1979.
Lesieutre, Alain, *The Spirit and Splendour of Art Deco*, London and New York 1974.
Logie, Gordon, *Furniture from Machines*, London 1947.
Makinson, Randell L., *Greene and Greene: Furniture and Related Designs*, Salt Lake City and Santa Barbara 1979.
Mang, Karl, *History of Modern Furniture*, London 1979.
Martinell, César, *Gaudí: His Life, His Theories, His Work*, Barcelona 1975.
Massobrio, Giovanna, and Portoghesi, Paolo, *La seggiola di Vienna: storia dei mobili in legno curvato*, Turin n.d.
McClinton, Katharine Morrison, *Art Deco: A Guide for Collectors*, New York 1972.
Meader, Robert, *An Illustrated Guide to Shaker Furniture*, New York 1972.
Meadmore, Clement, *The Modern Chair: Classics in Production*, New York 1979.
Nelson, George, *Chairs*, New York 1953.

Pevsner, Nikolaus, *Pioneers of Modern Design: From William Morris to Walter Gropius*, New York and Harmondsworth 1975.
Wilk, Christopher, *Marcel Breuer: Furniture and Interiors*, New York 1981.
Wingler, Hans M., *The Bauhaus: Weimar, Dessau, Berlin, Chicago*, Cambridge, Massachussetts 1969.

Catalogues

Aalto: Architecture and Furniture, Museum of Modern Art, New York 1938.
Alvar Aalto Furniture, Finnish Museum of Architecture, Helsinki 1984.
Art Nouveau: Art and Design at the Turn of the Century, Museum of Modern Art, New York 1959.
Art Nouveau Belgium, France, Institute for the Arts, Rice University and the Art Institute of Chicago 1976.
Bauhaus, Institut für Auslandsbeziehungen, Stuttgart 1975.
Cinquantenaire de l'Exposition de 1925, Musée des Arts Décoratifs, Paris 1976-77.
Ein Dokument Deutscher Kunst, Hessisches Landesmuseum 1976-77.
Charles Eames Furniture from the Design Collection of the Museum of Modern Art, New York 1973.
Furniture of Today: An Exhibition Presenting a Cross-Section of Modern Furniture Now Being Manufactured, Museum of Art, Rhode Island School of Design, Providence 1948.
Gebogenes Holz: Konstruktive Entwürfe Wien 1840-1910, Künstlerhaus Wien, Vienna 1979.
Ernest Gimson and the Cotswold Group of Craftsmen, catalogue of works by Ernest Gimson, Ernest and Sidney Barnsley and Peter Waals in the collections of Leicestershire Museums, Leicester 1978.
Eileen Gray: Designer 1879-1976, Victoria and Albert Museum, London, and Museum of Modern Art, New York 1979.
The Great Exhibition — London 1851: The Art-Journal Illustrated Catalogue of the Industries of All Nations, reprinted London 1970.
Josef Hoffmann Architect and Designer, Fischer Fine Art Ltd., London 1977.

Hoffmann, i 'mobili semplici' di Vienna 1900/1910, Galleria dell'Emporio Floreale n.d.
Introduction to Twentieth-Century Design from the Collection of the Museum of Modern Art, New York 1959.
Liberty's 1875-1975: An Exhibition to Mark the Firm's Centenary, Victoria and Albert Museum, London 1975.
Charles Rennie Mackintosh Furniture, Glasgow School of Art Collection, 1968.
Metalen Buisstoelen 1925-1940, Stedelijk Museum, Amsterdam 1975.
Ludwig Mies van der Rohe: Furniture and Furniture Drawings from the Design Collection and the Mies van der Rohe Archive, Museum of Modern Art, New York 1977.
Organic Design in Home Furnishings, Museum of Modern Art, New York 1941.
Pel and Tubular Steel Furniture of the Thirties, Architectural Association, London 1977.
The Shakers: Life and Production of a Community in the Pioneering Days of America, Neue Sammlung, Munich 1974.
300 Years of American Seating Furniture: Chairs and Beds from the Mabel Brady Garran and Other Collections at Yale University, Boston 1976.
Vienna at the Turn of the Century, Fischer Fine Art Ltd., London 1979.
C. F. A. Voysey Architect and Designer 1857-1941, Art Gallery and Museum, Brighton 1978.
Whitechapel Art Gallery London: Modern Chairs 1918-1970, catalogue of an international exhibition arranged by the Victoria and Albert Museum, London 1970.
Zwischen Kunst und Industrie: Der Deutsche Werkbund, Staatliches Museum für Angewandte Kunst, Munich 1975.

Miscellaneous

Art et Décoration.
Badovici, J., and Gray, E., *E-1027 Maison en Bord de Mer*, Paris n.d.
La Demeure Française.
Deshairs, Léon, *Une Ambassade Française*, Paris 1925.
Intérieurs Modernes en France, Paris n.d.
The Studio.

Photographic Acknowledgements

Thanks go to the following individuals and institutions for making material available for publication: A.C.L. Brussels 79.3; Albright-Knox Art Gallery, Buffalo, New York 51.8; T. & R. Annan 36.1; Aram Designs Limited 125.9, 136.8; Archives d'Architecture Moderne, Brussels 81.6; The Art Institute of Chicago 51.7; Art Workers Guild 43.4; Morely Baer, Monterey 32.5; Richard Ball 34.1, 127, 128; Bibliothèque Royale, Brussels 81.7; Cheltenham Museum and Art Gallery (Edward Barnsley collection) 19.4; City of Birmingham 49.2; Cooper-Hewitt Museum, Smithsonian Institution 38.1, 69.2, 70.10; The Design Council, London 146.3, 147, 149.4, 149.5, 149.6, 149.7 (Bugatti Family collection) 88.4, 88.5; Ediciones Poligrafa, Barcelona 90.3; Editions Graphiques, London 74.2; Escuela Tecnica Superior de Arquitectura de Barcelona 90.5; Fischer Fine Art Ltd., London 34.3, 34.4, 37.1, 37.2, 37.3, 59.2, 59.3; Foto Mas, Barcelona 90.4; Michael Freeman 51.3, 51.4, 51.5; Galerie du Luxembourg, Paris 71; Michael Graves 110.2; André Goulancourt 52.1; Haslam & Whiteway, London 14.1, 45.5; Thomas A. Heinz 51.6, 52.2; Leicester Museums and Art Galleries 14.2, 19.2, 19.3; Bill Maris 110.1; Macklowe Gallery, New York 91.1; Müncher Stadtmuseum, Munich 65.2, 65.3; Musée des Arts Décoratifs, Paris 70.5, 72.1, 74.1, 74.3, 74.4, 86.2, 96.1, 101.2, 101.3, 105.1, 108.7, 112.2, 112.3, 132.9, 132.10; Museum of Finnish Architecture (photo H. Havas) 143; Museum of Modern Art, New York 153.3, 153.4, 155 (Mies van der Rohe archives) 133; National Monuments Record, London 13 bottom, 88.3; Marvin Rand 32.2, 32.3, 32.4, 33.1, 33.2; Royal Academy of Arts, Piccadilly London 27.4; Sotheby's Belgravia London 21.3, 21.4, 25.5, 25.6, 25.7, 27.2, 34.2, 53, 75.6, 91.3, 101.6, 114.1, 125.11; Laurent Sully-Jaulmes 54, 70.8, 73, 87.2, 92, 97.2, 97.3, 101.4, 101.5, 101.7; Taylor & Dull Inc. 15.1; University of Glasgow (Mackintosh collection) 8, 48.7, 48.8; Victoria and Albert Museum, London 12.4, 13 top, 14.3, 16, 21.4, 22.2, 24.3, 24.4, 36.2, 44.3, 49.3, 88.3, 132.11, 132.12, 134.2, 138.3, 138.4, 139.6, 139.7, 139.8, 144.2, 146.2, 151.6, 153.5; Marc Vokaer 69.3, 70.4, 70.6, 70.7, 70.9; William Morris Gallery, Walthamstow 33.3, 33.4, 41.3.

Other material was taken from the following contemporary sources: *L'Architecture Vivante, L'Art Décoratif, Art et Décoration, La Demeure Moderne,* Deshairs, Léon *Une Ambassade Française, Deutsche Kunst und Dekoration, L'Illustration, The Studio.*

Index